Harry Levinson on the Psychology of Leadership

A Harvard Business Review Paperback

Copyright 2006 Harvard Business School Publishing Corporation
All rights reserved
Printed in the United States of America
10 09 08 07 06   5 4 3 2 1

978-1-4221-0205-3 (ISBN 13)

Library of Congress Cataloging-in-Publication Data

Levinson, Harry.
    Harry Levinson on the psychology of leadership.
        p. cm.—(A Harvard business review paperback)
    Includes index.
    ISBN 1-4221-0205-X
1. Leadership.   I. Title.   II. Title: On the psychology of leadership.
III. Series: Harvard business review paperback series
    HD57. 7.L4745 2006
    658.4'092019—dc22   2006013551

To Miriam Levinson,
steadfast supporter and loving partner

Contents

Introduction

Planning an issue of the *Harvard Business Review* is always a balancing act. We want to include articles based on cutting-edge research—but not at the expense of fully vetted practical advice. We want to publish the best-known management thinkers—but the magazine will become a relic unless we also find the most promising new researchers whose names aren't yet familiar to our readers. We look for articles that will appeal to all of our readers—and also first-rate work in specialized areas (and, let's face it, the CIOs among our readers won't always bother with the CMOs' must-read pieces). Most of all, we try to strike the right balance between articles that help managers solve immediate, pressing business needs and those that deepen their store of wisdom about management.

We're proud that so many of our articles have weathered the test of time; they enjoy a long afterlife as reprints and continue to get cited, years later, in the academic literature and in collections like the one you're about to read. We're often surprised by which ones make the cut: seemingly obscure articles about restructuring conglomerates in emerging markets are just as successful as more widely appealing articles on the psychology of leadership, for example. This is true in part because HBR is a hybrid publication; it inhabits the dual worlds of academic scholarship and practical management. Not only do the best researchers use our pages to reach a managerial audience, but so do ruthlessly practical management consultants. Our after markets, too, are fragmented: the articles that an HR vice president buys for professional development don't necessarily have much in common with the articles professors order for their MBA students. And the individual reader who buys a collection of reprints probably has something in common with both.

We have found, however, that our most long-lived articles do share three common traits. First, they're *original*. Authors who extend the work of others by an inch or two serve a worthy purpose—and we publish a lot of their ideas. But their thinking doesn't change the landscape of managerial practice in the way that, say, Peter Drucker, Harry Levinson, and Ted Levitt changed it. Second, the articles are *rigorous*. The work they contain is built on years of research or observation; as a result, they stand up over time. (Mind you, some of the best thinkers are highly intuitive, but they don't rush to publish their brilliant insight. They test it first.) And finally, the articles are *relevant*. They help managers do their work more effectively. We think you'll find this is true of the articles in this collection.

—SARAH CLIFFE, Executive Editor

1
Management by Whose Objectives?

In this 1970 classic HBR article, Levinson shares practical insights into the mysteries of motivation and takes a fresh look at the use and abuse of the most powerful tools for inspiring and guiding complex organizations. He argues that to motivate people successfully, management must focus on the question, "How do we meet both individual and organizational requirements?" When we make assumptions about individual motivations and increase pressure based on them, we ignore the fact that people work to meet their own psychological needs. Commitment must derive from the individual's wishes to support the organization's goals.

The performance appraisal systems that underpin MBO fail to take into account the deeper emotional components of motivation. Instead, managers are forced to commit to unrealistic goals. Superiors are profoundly uncomfortable rating people on performance, and they execute this important task poorly. The individual's desires are entirely absent from most performance measurement systems; managers assume that these desires are perfectly aligned with corporate goals and that if they're not, the individual should move on.

Self-motivation occurs when individual needs and organizational requirements converge. However, successful management systems begin with the *employee's* objectives. The manager's task is to understand the employee's needs and then, with the employee, assess how well the organization can meet them. Objectives lack significant incentive power if they are unrelated to employees' underlying personal aspirations. Management should give more weight to areas of discretion open to the individual but not officially incorporated into job descriptions or goals. Otherwise, a person may objectively do an excellent job but still fail as a partner, subordinate, superior, or colleague.

Despite the fact that the concept of management by objectives (MBO) has by this time become an integral part of the managerial process, the typical MBO effort perpetuates and intensifies hostility, resentment, and distrust between a manager and subordinates. As currently practiced, it is really just industrial engineering with a new name, applied to higher managerial levels, and with the same resistances intact.

Obviously, somewhere between the concept of MBO and its implementation, something has seriously gone wrong. Coupled with performance appraisal, the intent is to follow the Frederick Taylor tradition of a more rational management process. That is, which people are to do what, who is to have effective control over the process, and how compensation is to be related directly to individual achievement. The MBO process, in its essence, is an effort to be fair and reasonable, to predict performance and judge it more carefully, and presumably to provide individuals with an opportunity to be self-motivating by setting their own objectives.

The intent of clarifying job obligations and measuring performance against an employee's own goals seems reasonable enough. The concern for having superior and subordinate consider the same matters in reviewing the performance of the latter is eminently sensible. The effort to come to common agreement on what constitutes the subordinate's job is highly desirable.

Yet, like most rationalizations in the Taylor tradition, MBO as a process is one of the greatest of managerial illusions because it fails to take adequately into account the deeper emotional components of motivation.

In this article, I shall indicate how I think management by objectives, as it is currently practiced in most organizations, is self-defeating and serves simply to increase pressure on the individual. By doing so, I am not rejecting either MBO or performance appraisal out of hand.

Rather, by raising the basic question, "Whose objectives?" I propose to suggest how they might be made into more constructive devices for effective management. The issues I shall raise have largely to do with psychological considerations, and particularly with the assumptions about motivation that underlie these techniques.

The "Ideal" Process

Because management by objectives is closely related to performance appraisal and review, I shall consider these together as one practice, which is intended:

- To measure and judge performance,
- To relate individual performance to organizational goals,
- To clarify both the job to be done and the expectations of accomplishment,
- To foster the increasing competence and growth of the subordinate,
- To enhance communications between superior and subordinate,
- To serve as a basis for judgments about salary and promotion,
- To stimulate the subordinate's motivation, and
- To serve as a device for organizational control and integration.

MAJOR PROBLEMS

According to contemporary thinking, the "ideal" process should proceed in five steps:

1. individual discussion with the superior of the subordinate's own job description,
2. establishment of the employee's short-term performance targets,
3. meetings with the superior to discuss the employee's progress toward targets,
4. establishment of checkpoints to measure progress, and
5. discussion between superior and subordinate at the end of a defined period to assess the results of the subordinate's efforts.

In ideal practice, this process occurs against a background of more frequent, even day-to-day, contacts and is separate from salary review. But, in actual practice, there are many problems.

No matter how detailed the job description, it is essentially static—that is, a series of statements. However, the more complex the task and the more flexible an employee must be in it, the less any fixed statement of job elements will fit what that person does. Thus, the higher a person rises in an organization and the more varied and subtle the work, the more difficult it is to pin down objectives that represent more than a fraction of his or her effort.

With preestablished goals and descriptions, little weight can be given to the areas of discretion open to the individual but not incorporated into a job description or objectives. I am referring here to those spontaneously creative activities an innovative executive might choose to do, or those tasks a responsible executive sees need to be done. As we move toward a service society, in which tasks are less well defined but spontaneity of service and self-assumed responsibility are crucial, this becomes pressing.

Most job descriptions are limited to what employees do in their work. They do not adequately take into account the increasing interdependence of managerial work in organizations. This limitation becomes more important as the impact of social and organizational factors on individual performance becomes better understood. The more employees' effectiveness depends on what other people do, the less any one employee can be held responsible for the outcome of individual efforts.

If a primary concern in performance review is counseling the subordinate, appraisal should consider and take into account the total situation in which the superior and subordinate are operating. In addition, this should take into account the relationship of the subordinate's job to other jobs. In counseling, much of the focus is on helping the subordinate learn to negotiate the system. There is no provision in most reviews and no place on appraisal forms with which I am familiar to report and record such discussion.

The setting and evolution of objectives is done over too brief a period of time to provide for adequate interaction among different levels of an organization. This militates against opportunity for peers, both in the same work unit and in complementary units, to develop objectives together for maximum integration. Thus, both the setting of objectives and the appraisal of performance make little contribution to the development of teamwork and more effective organizational self-control.

Coupled with these problems is the difficulty that superiors experience when they undertake appraisals. Douglas McGregor complained that the major reason appraisal failed was that superiors disliked playing God by making judgments about another person's worth.[1] He likened the superior's experience to inspection of assembly-line products and contended that his revulsion was against being inhuman. To cope with this problem, McGregor recommended that an individual should set his or her own goals, checking them out with the superior, and should use the appraisal session as a counseling device. Thus, the superior would become one who helped subordinates achieve their own goals instead of a dehumanized inspector of products.

Parenthetically, I doubt very much that the failure of appraisal stems from playing God or feeling inhuman. My own observation leads me to believe that managers experience their appraisal of others as a hostile, aggressive act that unconsciously is felt to be hurting or destroying the other person. The appraisal situation, therefore, gives rise to powerful, paralyzing feelings of guilt that make it extremely difficult for most executives to be constructively critical of subordinates.

OBJECTIVITY PLEA

Be that as it may, the more complex and difficult the appraisal process and the setting and evaluation of objectives, the more pressing the cry for objectivity. This is a vain plea. Every organization is a social system, a network of interpersonal relationships. A person may do an excellent job by objective standards of measurement, but may fail miserably as a partner, subordinate, superior, or colleague. It is a commonplace that more people fail to be promoted for personal reasons than for technical inadequacy.

Furthermore, because all subordinates are a component of their superiors' efforts to achieve their own goals, subordinates will inevitably be appraised on how well they work with superiors and help the latter meet goals. A heavy subjective element necessarily enters into every appraisal and goal-setting experience.

The plea for objectivity is made in vain for another reason. The greater the emphasis placed on measurement and quantification, the more likely the subtle, nonmeasurable elements of the task will be sacrificed. Quality of performance frequently, therefore, loses out to quantification.

A case example: One manufacturing plant that produces high-quality, high-prestige products, backed by a reputation for customer consideration and service, has instituted an MBO program. It is well worked out and has done much to clarify individual goals and organizational performance. It is an important component of the professional management style of that company, which has resulted in commendable growth.

But an interesting, and ultimately destructive, process has been set in motion. The managers are beginning to worry because now when they ask why something has not been done, they hear from one another, "That isn't in my goals." They complain that customer service is deteriorating. The vague goal, "improve customer service," is almost impossible to measure. There is therefore heavy concentration on those subgoals that can be measured. Thus, time per customer, number of customer calls, and similar measures are used as guides in judging performance. The less time per customer and the fewer the calls, the better the customer service manager meets his objectives. He is cutting costs, increasing profit—and killing the business. Worse still, he hates himself.

Most of the managers in that organization joined it because of its reputation for high quality and good service. They want to make good products and earn the continued admiration of their customers, as well as the envy of their industry. When they are not operating at that high level, they feel guilty. They become angry with themselves and the company. They feel that they might just as well be working for someplace else that admittedly does a sloppy job of quality control and could hardly care less about service.

The same problem exists with respect to the development of personnel, which is another vague goal that is hard to measure in comparison with subgoals that are measurable. If asked, each manager can name a younger employee as a potential successor, particularly if a promotion depends on doing so; but no one has the time, or indeed is being paid, to thoroughly train the younger person. Nor can one have the time or be paid, for there is no way in that organization to measure how well a manager does in developing another.

The Missed Point

All of the problems with objectives and appraisals outlined in the example discussed in the foregoing section indicate that MBO is not working well despite what some companies think about their programs. The underlying reason it is not working well is that it misses the whole human point.

To see how the point is being missed, let us follow the typical MBO process. Characteristically, top management sets its corporate goal for the coming year. This may be in terms of return on investment, sales, production, growth, or other measurable factors.

Within this frame of reference, reporting managers may then be asked how much their units intend to contribute toward meeting that goal, or they may be asked to set their own goals relatively independent of the corporate goal. If they are left free to set their own goals, these in any case are expected to be higher than those they had the previous year. Usually, each reporting manager's range of choices is limited to an option for a piece of the organizational action or improvement of specific statistics. In some cases, it may also include obtaining specific training or skills.

Once a reporting manager decides on the unit's goals and has them approved by his superior, those become the manager's goals. Presumably, he has committed himself to what he wants to do. He has said it and he is responsible for it. He is thereafter subject to being hoisted with his own petard.

Now, let us reexamine this process closely: The whole method is based on a short-term, egocentrically oriented perspective and an underlying reward-punishment psychology. The typical MBO process puts the reporting manager in much the same position as a rat in a maze, which has choices between only two alternatives. The experimenter who puts the rat in the maze assumes that the rat will choose the food reward. If that cannot be presumed, the rat is starved to make sure it wants the food.

Management by objectives differs only in that it permits the manager to determine his or her own bait from a limited range of choices. Having done so, the MBO process assumes that the manager will a) work hard to get it, b) be pushed internally by reason of this commitment, and c) be responsible to the organization for doing so.

In fairness to most managers, they certainly try, but not without increasing resentment and complaint for feeling like rats in a maze, guilt for not paying attention to those parts of the job not in their objectives, and passive resistance to the mounting pressure for ever-higher goals.

PERSONAL GOALS

The MBO process leaves out the answers to such questions as: What are the managers' personal objectives? What do they need and want out of their work? How do their needs and wants change from year to year? What relevance do organizational objectives and their part in them have to such needs and wants?

Obviously, no objectives will have significant incentive power if they are forced choices unrelated to a person's underlying dreams, wishes, and personal aspirations.

For example: If a salesperson relishes the pleasure of his relationships with his hard-earned but low-volume customers, this is a powerful need for him. Suppose his boss, who is concerned about increasing the volume of sales, urges him to concentrate on the larger-quantity customers rather than the smaller ones, which will provide the necessary increase in volume, and then asks him how much of an increase he can achieve.

To work with the larger-quantity customers means that he will be less likely to sell to the individuals with whom he has well-established relationships and be more likely to deal with purchasing agents, technical people, and staff specialists who will demand of him knowledge and information he may not have in sophisticated detail. Moreover, as a single salesperson, his organization may fail to support him with technical help to meet these demands.

When this happens, not only may he lose his favorite way of operating, which has well served his own needs, but he may have demands put on him that cause him to feel inadequate. If he is being compelled to make a choice about the percent of sales volume increase he expects to attain, he may well do that, but now he's under great psychological pressure. No one has recognized the psychological realities he faces, let alone helped him to work with them. It is simply assumed that because his sales goal is a rational one, he will see its rationality and pursue it.

The problem may be further compounded if, as is not unusual, formal changes are made in the organizational structure. If sales territories are shifted, if problems of delivery occur, if modes of compensation are changed, or whatever, all of these are factors beyond the salesperson's control. Nevertheless, even with certain allowances, he is still held responsible for meeting his sales goal.

PSYCHOLOGICAL NEEDS

Lest the reader think that the example we have just seen is overdrawn or irrelevant, I know of a young sales manager who is about to resign his job, despite success in it, because he chooses not to be expendable in an organization that he feels regards him only as an instrument for reaching a goal. Many young people are refusing to enter large organizations for just this reason.

Some may argue that my criticism is unfair, that many organizations start their planning and setting of objectives from below. Therefore, the company cannot be accused of putting a person in a maze. But it does so. In almost all cases, the only legitimate objectives to be set are those having to do with measurable increases in performance. This highlights, again, the question, "Whose objectives?" The question becomes more pressing in those circumstances where lower-level people set their objectives, only to be questioned by higher-level managers and told their targets are not high enough.

You may well ask, "What's the matter with that? Aren't we in business, and isn't the purpose of the employee's work to serve the requirements of the business?" The answer to both questions is, "Obviously." But that is only part of the story.

If a person's most powerful driving force is comprised of needs, wishes, and personal aspirations, combined with the compelling wish to look good in her own eyes for meeting those deeply held personal goals, then management by objectives should begin with *her* objectives. What does she want to do with her life? Where does she want to go? What will make her feel good about herself? What does she want to be able to look back on when she has expended her unrecoverable years?

At this point, some may say that those are her business. The company has other business, and it must assume that the employee is interested in working in the company's business rather than her own. That kind of differentiation is impossible. Everyone is always working toward meeting his or her psychological needs. Anyone who thinks otherwise, and who believes such powerful internal forces can be successfully disregarded or bought off for long, is deluded.

The Mutual Task

The organizational task becomes one of first understanding the employee's needs, and then, with him or her, assessing how well they can be met in this organization, doing what the organization needs to have done. Thus, the highest point of self-motivation arises when there is a complementary conjunction of the individual's needs and the organization's requirements. The requirements of both mesh, interrelate, and become synergistic. The energies of employee and organization are pooled for mutual advantage.

If the two sets of needs do not mesh, then a person has to fight him- or herself and the organization, in addition to the work that must be done and the targets that have been defined. In such a case, this requires the subordinate and the boss to evaluate together where the employee wants to go, where the organization is going, and how significant the discrepancy is. This person might well be better off somewhere else, and the organization would do better to have someone else in place whose needs mesh better with the organization's requirements.

LONG-RUN COSTS

The issue of meshed interests is particularly relevant for middle-aged, senior-level managers.[2] As people come into middle age, their values often begin to change, and they feel anew the pressure to accomplish many long-deferred dreams. When such wishes begin to stir, they begin to experience severe conflict.

Up to this point, they have committed themselves to the organization and have done sufficiently well in it to attain high rank. Usually, they are slated for even higher levels of responsibility. The organization has been good to them, and their superiors are depending on them to provide its leadership. They have been models for the younger employees, whom they have urged to aspire to organizational heights. To think of leaving is to desert both their superiors and their subordinates.

Because there are few avenues within the organization to talk about such conflict, these managers try to suppress their wishes. The internal pressure continues to mount until they finally make an impulsive break, surprising and dismaying both themselves and their colleagues. I can think of three vice presidents who have done just that.

The issue is not so much that they decide to leave, but the cost of the way they depart. Early discussion with superiors of their personal goals would have enabled both to examine possible relocation alternatives within the organization. If there were none, then both the managers and their superiors might have come to an earlier, more comfortable decision about separation. The organization would have had more time to make satisfactory alternative plans, as well as to have taken steps to compensate for the manager's lagging enthusiasm. Lower-level managers would then have seen the company as humane in its enlightened self-interest and would not have had to create fearful fantasies about what the top management conflicts were that had caused a good person to leave.

To place consideration of the managers' personal objectives first does not minimize the importance of the organization's goals. It does not mean there is anything wrong with the organization's need to increase its return on investment, its size, its productivity, or its other goals. However, I contend that it is ridiculous to make assumptions about the motivations of individuals, and then to set up means of increasing the pressures on people based on these often questionable assumptions. While there may be certain demonstrable short-run statistical gains, what are the long-run costs?

One cost is that people may leave; another, that they may fall back from competitive positions to plateaus. Why should an individual be expendable for someone else and sacrifice for something that is not a personal, cherished dream? Still another cost may be the loss of the essence of the business, as happened in the case example we saw earlier of the manufacturing plant with the problem of deteriorating customer service.

In that example, initially there was no dialogue. Nobody heard what the managers said, what they wanted, where they wanted to go, where they wanted the organization to go, and how they felt about the supposedly rational procedures that had been initiated. The underlying psychological assumption that management made unconsciously was that the managers had to be made more efficient; ergo, management by objectives.

Top management typically assumes that it alone has the prerogative to a) set the objectives, b) provide the rewards and targets, and c) drive anyone who works for the organization. As long as this reward-punishment psychology exists in any organization, the MBO appraisal process is certain to fail.

Many organizations are making this issue worse by promising young people they will have challenges because they assume these employees will be challenged by management's objectives. Managements are having difficulty, even when they have high turnover rates, hearing these youngsters say they could hardly care less for management's unilaterally determined objectives. Managements then become angry and complain that the young people do not want to work or that they want to become presidents overnight.

What the young people are asking is: What about me and my needs? Who will listen? How much will management help me meet my own requirements while also meeting its objectives?

The power of this force is reflected in the finding that the more a subordinate participates in the appraisal interview by presenting personal ideas and beliefs, the more likely he or she is to feel that a) the superior is helpful and constructive, b) some current job problems are being cleared up, and c) reasonable future goals are being set.[3]

Suggested Steps

Given the validity of all the MBO problems I have been discussing to this point, there are a number of possibilities for coping with them. Here, I suggest three beginning steps to consider.

MOTIVATIONAL ASSESSMENT

Every MBO program and its accompanying performance appraisal system should be examined as to the extent to which it a) expresses the conviction that people are patsies to be driven, urged, and manipulated, and b) fosters a genuine partnership between employee and organization, in which each has some influence over the other, as contrasted with a rat-in-maze relationship.

It is not easy for the nonpsychologist to answer such questions, but there are clues to the answers. One clue is how decisions about compensation, particularly bonuses, are made. For example: A sales manager asked for my judgment about an incentive plan for highly motivated salespeople who were in a seller's market. I asked why one was needed, and he responded, "To give them an incentive." When I pointed out that they were already highly motivated and apparently needed no incentive, he changed his rationale and said that the company wanted to share its success to keep the sales staff identified with it, and to express its recognition of their contribution.

I asked, "Why not let them establish the reward related to performance?" The question startled him; obviously, if they were going to decide, who needed him? A fundamental aspect of his role, as he saw it, was to drive them ever onward, whether they needed it or not.

In a plastic-fabricating company, a middle-management bonus plan tied to performance proved to be highly unsatisfactory. Frustrated that its well-intentioned efforts were not working and determined to follow precepts of participative management, ranking executives in the company involved many people in formulating a new one: personnel, control, marketing executives, and others—in fact, everyone but the managers who were supposed to receive the bonuses. Top management is now dismayed that the new plan is as unsatisfactory as the old and bitter that participation failed to work.

Another clue is the focus of company meetings. Some are devoted to intensifying the competition between units. Others lean heavily to exhortation and inspiration. Contrast these orientations with meetings in which people are apprised of problems and plan to cope with them.

GROUP ACTION

Every objectives and appraisal program should include group goal setting, group definition of individual and group tasks, group appraisal of its accomplishments, group appraisal of each individual member's contribution to the group effort (without basing compensation on that appraisal), and shared compensation based on the relative success with which group goals are achieved. Objectives should include long-term as well as short-term goals.

The rationale is simple. Every managerial job is an interdependent task. Managers have responsibilities to one another as well as to their superiors. The reason for having an organization is to achieve more together than each could alone. Why, then, emphasize and reward individual performance alone, based on static job descriptions? That approach can only orient people to incorrect and self-centered goals.

Therefore, where people are in complementary relationships, whether they report to the same superior or not, both horizontal and vertical goal formulation should be formalized, with regular, frequent opportunity for review of problems and progress. They should help one another define and describe their respective jobs, enhancing control and integration at the point of action.

In my judgment, for example, a group of managers (sales, promotion, advertising) reporting to a vice president of marketing should formulate their collective goals and define ways of helping one another and of assessing one another's effectiveness in the common task. The group assessment of each manager's work should be a means of providing each one with constructive feedback, not for determining pay. However, in addition to their salaries, they should each receive, as part of whatever additional compensation is offered, a return based on the group effort.

The group's discussion among itself and with its superior should include examination of organizational and environmental obstacles to goal achievement, and particularly of what organizational and leadership supports are required to attain objectives. One important reason for this is that often people think there are barriers where none would exist if they initiated action. ("You mean the president really wants us to get together and solve this problem?")

Another reason is that frequently when higher management sets goals, it is unaware of significant barriers to achievement, which makes managers cynical. For example, if there is no comprehensive orientation and support program to help new employees adapt, then pressure on lower-level managers to employ disadvantaged minority group members and to reduce their turnover can only be experienced by those managers as hollow mockery.

APPRAISAL OF APPRAISERS

Every management by objectives and appraisal program should include regular appraisals of the manager by subordinates, and be reviewed by the manager's superior. Every manager should be specifically compensated for how well he or she develops people, based on such appraisals. The very phrase "reporting to" reflects the fact that although a manager has a responsibility, the superior also has a responsibility for what he or she does and how it's done.

In fact, both common sense and research indicate that the single most significant outside influence on how a manager performs is the superior. If that is the case, then the key environmental factor in task accomplishment and managerial growth is the relationship between manager and superior.

Therefore, objectives should include not only the individual manager's personal and occupational goals, but also the corporate goals manager and superior share in common. They should together appraise their relationship vis-à-vis both the manager's individual goals and their joint objectives, review what they have done together, and discuss its implications for their next joint steps.

A manager rarely is in a position to judge a superior's overall performance, but he or she can appraise how well the superior has helped the manager to do the job, how well the superior is helping to increase the manager's proficiency and visibility, what problems the superior poses for the manager, and what kinds of support the superior can use. Such feedback serves several purposes.

Most important, it offers some guidance on the superior's own managerial performance. In addition, and particularly when the manager is protected by higher-level review of this appraisal, it provides the supervisor with direct feedback on his or her own behavior. This is much more constructive than behind-the-back complaints and vituperative terminal interviews, in which cases there is no opportunity either for self-defense or corrective behavior. Every professional counselor has had recently fired executive clients who did not know why they had been discharged for being poor superiors when, according to their information, their subordinates thought so much of them. In his or her own self-interest, every manager should want appraisal by subordinates.

The Basic Consideration

When the three organizational conditions we have just seen do in fact exist, then it is appropriate to think of starting management by objectives with a consideration of each employee's personal objectives; if the underlying attitude in the organization toward the subordinate is that he or she is but an object, there is certainly no point in starting with the person. Nor is there any point in trying to establish confidence in superiors when there is no protection from their rivalry, or being pitted against peers. Anyone who expressed personal fears and innermost wishes under these circumstances would be a damned fool.

For reasons I have already indicated, it should be entirely legitimate in every business for these concerns to be the basis for setting individual objectives. This is because the fundamental managerial consideration necessarily must be focused on the question: "How do we meet both individual and organizational purposes?" If a major intention of management by objectives is to enlist the self-motivated commitment of the individual, then that commitment must derive from the individual's powerful wishes to support the organization's goals; otherwise, the commitment will be incidental to any personal wishes.

Having said that, the real difficulty begins. How can any superior know what a subordinate's personal goals and wishes are if even the subordinate—as most of us are—is not clear about them? How ethical is it for a superior to pry into an employee's personal life? How can he or she keep from forming a negative judgment about someone who is losing interest in work, or is not altogether identified with the company? How can the superior keep that knowledge from interfering with judgments he or she might otherwise make, and opportunities he or she might otherwise offer? How often are the personal goals, particularly in middle age, temporary fantasies that are better not discussed? Can a superior who is untrained in psychology handle such information constructively? Will he or she perhaps do more harm than good?

These are critically important questions. They deserve careful thought. My answers should be taken as no more than beginning steps.

EGO CONCEPTS

Living is a process of constant adaptation. An individual's personal goals, wishes, and aspirations are continuously evolving and being continuously modified by experiences. That is one reason why it is so difficult for an individual to specify concrete personal objectives.

Nevertheless, each of us has a built-in road map, a picture of his or her future best self. Psychologists speak of this as an *ego ideal,* which is comprised of a person's values, the expectations parents and others have held out for competences and skills, and favorite ways of behaving. An ego ideal is essentially the way an individual thinks he or she ought to be. Much of a person's ego ideal is unconscious, which is another reason why it is not clear.

Subordinates' self-examination: Although people cannot usually spell out their ego ideal, they can talk about those experiences that have been highly gratifying, even exhilarating. They can specify those rare peak experiences that made them feel very good about themselves. When they have an opportunity to talk about what they have found especially gratifying and also what they think would be gratifying to them, people are touching on central elements of their ego ideal.

Given the opportunity to talk about such experiences and wishes on successive occasions, people can begin to spell out for themselves the central thrust of their lives. Reviewing all of the occupational choices they have made and the reasons for making them, people can begin to see the common threads in those choices and therefore the momentum of their personalities. As these become clearer, they are in a better position to weigh alternatives against the mainstream of their personalities.

For example, an individual who has successively chosen occupational alternatives in which she was individually competitive, and whose most exhilarating experiences have come from defeating an opponent or single-handedly vanquishing a problem, would be unlikely to find a staff position exhilarating, no matter what it paid or what it was called. Her ideal for herself is that of a vanquishing, competitive person.

The important concept here is that it is not necessary that an individual spell out concrete goals at any one point; rather, it is helpful to both the individual and the organization if he or she is able to examine and review aloud on a continuing basis personal thoughts and feelings in relation to his or her work. Such a process makes it legitimate to bring his or her own feelings to consciousness and talk about them in the business context as the basis for a relationship to the organization.

By listening, and helping the subordinate to spell out how and what he or she feels, the superior does not do anything to the subordinate, and therefore by that self-appraisal process cannot be hurtful. The information serves both employee and superior as a criterion for examining the relationship of the employee's feelings and, however dimly perceived, personal goals to organizational goals. Even if some of these wishes and aspirations are mere fantasy and impossible to gratify, if it is legitimate to talk about them without being laughed at, the individual can compare them with the realities of his or her life and make more reasonable choices.

Even in the safest organizational atmosphere, for reasons already mentioned, it will not be easy for managers to talk about their goals. The best-intentioned supervisor is likely to be something less than a highly skilled interviewer. These two facts suggest that any effort to ascertain a subordinate's personal goals is futile; but I think not.

The important point is not the specificity of the statement that any person can make, but the nature of a superior-subordinate relationship that makes it safe to explore such feelings and gives first consideration to the individual. In such a context, both subordinate and superior may come closer to evolving an employee-organization fit than they might otherwise.

Superior's introspection: An employee-organization relationship requires the superior to engage in some introspection, too. Suppose he has prided himself on bringing along a bright young manager who, he now learns, is thinking of moving into a different field. How can he keep from being angry and disappointed? How can he cope with the conflict he now faces when it is time to make recommendations for advancement or a raise?

The superior cannot keep from being angry and disappointed. Such feelings are natural in that circumstance. He can express feelings of disappointment to his protégé without being critical of the latter. But, if he continues to feel angry, then he needs to ask himself why another person's assertion of independence irritates him so. The issues of advancement and raises should continue to be based on the same realistic premises as they would have been before.

Of course, it now becomes appropriate to consider with the individual whether—in view of his feelings—he wants to take on the burden of added responsibility and can reasonably discharge it. If he thinks he does, and can, he is likely to pursue the new responsibility with added determination. With his occupational choice conflict no longer hidden, and with fewer feelings of guilt about it, his commitment to his chosen alternative is likely to be more intense.

And if an employee has earned a raise, he or she should get it. To withhold it merely punishes him or her, which puts the relationship back on a reward-punishment basis.

The question of how ethical it is to conduct such discussions as part of a business situation hinges on the climate of the organization and on the sense of personal responsibility of each executive. Where the organization's ethos is one of building trust and keeping confidences, there is no reason why executives cannot be as ethical as lawyers or physicians.

If the individual executive cannot be trusted in relationships with subordinates, then he or she cannot have their respect or confidence in any case, and the ordinary MBO appraisal process simply serves as a management pressure device. If the organization's ethos is one of rapacious internal competition, backbiting, and distrust, there is little point in talking about self-motivation, human needs, or commitment.

Management by objectives and performance appraisal processes, as typically practiced, are inherently self-defeating over the long run because they are based on a reward-punishment psychology that serves to intensify the pressure on the individual while really offering a very limited choice of objectives. Such processes can be improved by examining the psychological assumptions underlying them, by extending them to include group appraisal and appraisal of superiors by subordinates, and by considering the personal goals of the individual first. These practices require a high level of ethical standards and personal responsibility in the organization.

Such appraisal processes would diminish the feeling on the part of the superior that appraisal is a hostile, destructive act. While superior and subordinate would still have to judge the latter's individual performance, this judgment would occur in a context of continuing consideration for personal needs and reappraisal of organizational and environmental realities.

Not having to be continuously on the defensive and aware of the organization's genuine interest in having him or her meet personal as well as organizational goals, a manager would be freer to evaluate him- or herself against what has to be done. Because there would be many additional frames of reference in both horizontal and vertical goal setting, the manager would need no longer feel under appraisal, attack, or judgment as an isolated individual against the system. Furthermore, there would be multiple modes for contributing ideas and a varied method for exerting influence upward and horizontally.

In these contexts, too, the manager could raise questions and concerns about qualitative aspects of performance. Then manager, colleagues, and superiors could together act to cope with such issues without the barrier of having to consider only statistics. Thus, a continuing process of interchange would counteract the problem of the static job description and provide multiple avenues for feedback on performance and joint action.

In such an organizational climate, work relationships would then become dynamic networks for both personal and organizational achievements. A not-incidental gain from such arrangements is that problems would more likely be solved spontaneously at the lowest possible levels, and free superiors simultaneously from the burden of the passed buck and the onus of being the purveyors of hostility.

Notes

1. "An Uneasy Look at Performance Appraisal," HBR May–June 1957, p. 89. (Reprinted as an HBR Classic, September–October 1972.)
2. See my article, "On Being a Middle-Aged Manager," HBR July–August 1969, p. 51.
3. Ronald J. Burke and Douglas S. Wilcox, "Characteristics of Effective Employee Performance Reviews and Developmental Interviews," *Personal Psychology,* Vol. 22, No. 3, 1969, p. 291.

Reprint R0301H

Originally published in 1970, republished in January 2003.

2
When Executives Burn Out

The military knows about burnout—but calls it battle fatigue. To offset its devastating effects, the military routinely schedules its personnel for recreation and relaxation retreats, sends soldiers into combat in groups so they can support and help each other, and limits the number of flights that pilots fly. Managers are not soldiers but, according to this author and others who have researched the subject, they are prone to a similar exhaustion and sense of futility. Like other professionals, mental health workers, and policemen who work under severe pressure in people-oriented jobs for long periods of time—with little support and limited gains—managers are among the prime victims of burnout. The author describes what burnout is, discusses why he thinks that modern organizations are good breeding grounds for situations that lead to it, and offers some helpful ways top managers can combat it.

"I just can't seem to get going," the vice president said. He grimaced as he leaned back in his chair. "I can't get interested in what I'm supposed to do. I know I should get rolling. I know there's a tremendous amount of work to be done. That's why they brought me in and put me in this job, but I just can't seem to get going."

Eighteen months before making these comments, the vice president had transferred to company headquarters from a subsidiary. His new job was to revamp the company's control systems, which, because of a reorganization, were in disarray. When the vice president reported to headquarters, however, top management immediately recruited him to serve as a key staff figure in its own reshuffling. Because he was not in competition with line executives, he was the only staff person who interviewed and consulted with both the line executives and the chief executive officer. And because the top managers regarded him as trustworthy, they gave his recommendations serious attention.

But his task had been arduous. Not only did the long hours and the unremitting pressure of walking a tightrope among conflicting interests exhaust him; they also made it impossible for him to get at the control problems that needed attention. Furthermore, because his family could not move until his youngest child finished high school, he commuted on weekends to his family's home 800 miles away. As he tried to perform the job that had been thrust on him and to support the CEO, who was counting heavily on his competence, he felt lonely, harassed, and burdened. Now that his staff responsibilities were coming to an end, he was in no psychological shape to take on his formal duties. In short, he had "burned out."

Like generalized stress, burnout cuts across executive and managerial levels. While the phenomenon manifests itself in varying ways and to different degrees in different people, it appears nonetheless to have identifiable characteristics. For instance, in the next example, the individual is different but many of the features of the problem are the same.

A vice president of a large corporation who hadn't received an expected promotion left his company to become the CEO of a smaller, family-owned business, which was floundering and needed his skills. Although he had jumped at the opportunity to rescue the small company, once there he discovered an unimaginable morass of difficulties, among them continual conflicts within the family. He felt he could not leave, but neither could he succeed. Trapped in a kind of psychological quicksand, he worked days, nights, and weekends for months in an attempt to pull himself free. His wife protested, to no avail. Finally, he was hospitalized for exhaustion.

As in the previous example, the competence of the individual is not in question; today he is the chief executive of a major corporation.

Quite a different set of problems confronted another executive. This is how he tells his story:

"In March of 1963, I moved to a small town in Iowa with my wife and son of four weeks. I was an up-and-coming engineer with the electric company—magic and respected words in those days.

"Ten years later, things had changed. When we went to social gatherings and talked to people, I ended up having to defend the electric company. At the time, we were tying into a consortium that was building a nuclear generating plant. The amount of negative criticism was immense, and it never really let up. Refusing to realize how important that generating plant was to a reliable flow of electricity, people continued to find fault.

"Now, nearly ten years later, we are under even greater attack. In my present role, I'm the guy who catches it all. I can't seem to get people to stand still and listen, and I can't continue to take all the hostility that goes with it—the crank calls, being woken up late at night and called names. I don't know how much longer I can last in this job."

Before looking in depth at what the phenomenon of burnout is, let's look at the experience of one more executive who is well on his way to burning out:

"I have been with this company for nearly 15 years and have changed jobs every 2 to 3 years. Most of our managers are company men, like me. We have always been a high-technology company, but we have been doing less well in marketing than some of our competitors have. Over the past 10 years, we have been going through a continuous reorganization process. The organization charts keep changing, but the underlying philosophy, management techniques, and administrative trappings don't. The consequence is continuous frustration, disruption, resentment, and the undermining of 'change.' You don't take a company that has been operating with a certain perspective and turn it around overnight.

"With these changes, we are also being told what we must do and when. Before, we were much more flexible and free to follow our noses. These shifts create enormous pressures on an organization that is used to different ways of operating.

"On top of that, a continual corporate pruning goes on. I am a survivor, so I should feel good about it and believe what top management tells me, namely, that the unfit go and the worthy remain. But the old virtues—talent, initiative, and risk taking—are *not* being rewarded. Instead, acquiescence to corporate values and social skills that obliterate differences among individuals are the virtues that get attention. Also, the reward process is more political than meritocratic.

"I don't know if we're going to make it. And there are a lot of others around here who have the same feeling. We're all demoralized."

Burnout—A Slow Fizzle

What was happening to these executives? In exploring that question, let's first look at what characterized the situations. In one or more cases, the situations

- were repetitive or prolonged;
- placed enormous burdens on the managers;
- promised great success but made attaining it nearly impossible;
- exposed the managers to risk of attack for doing their jobs, without providing a way for them to fight back;
- aroused deep emotions—sorrow, fear, despair, compassion, helplessness, pity, and rage; to survive, the managers would try to contain their feelings and hide their anguish;
- overwhelmed the managers with complex detail, conflicting forces, and problems against which they hurled themselves with increasing intensity but without impact;
- exploited the managers but provided them little to show for having been victimized;
- aroused an inescapable sense of inadequacy and often of guilt;
- left the managers feeling that no one knew, let alone gave a damn about, what price they were paying, what contribution or sacrifice they were making, or what punishment they were absorbing;
- caused the managers to raise the question What for?—as if they'd lost sight of the purpose of living.

Those who study cases like these agree that a special phenomenon occurs after people expend a great deal of effort, intense to the point of exhaustion, without visible results. People in these situations feel angry, helpless, trapped, and depleted: they are burned out. This experience is more intense than what is ordinarily referred to as stress. The major defining characteristic of burnout is that people can't or won't do again what they have been doing.

Herbert J. Freudenberger, a New York psychologist, evolved this characterization of burnout when he observed a special sort of fatigue among mental health workers.[1] Freudenberger observed that burnout is associated with physiological signs such as frequent headaches and the inability to shake colds, as well as with psychological symptoms such as quickness to anger and a suspicious attitude about others.

Christina Maslach, a pioneer researcher on the subject at the University of California at Berkeley, says that burnout "refers to a syndrome of emotional exhaustion and cynicism that frequently occurs among people who do 'people work'—who spend considerable time in close encounters."[2]

People suffering from burnout generally have these identifiable characteristics: (1) chronic fatigue; (2) anger at those making demands;

(3) self-criticism for putting up with the demands; (4) cynicism, negativity, and irritability; (5) a sense of being besieged; and (6) hair-trigger display of emotions.

Although it is not evident from the above examples, a wide range of behaviors—some of them destructive—frequently accompany these feelings. Burned-out managers may inappropriately vent anger at subordinates and family, or withdraw even from those whose support they need the most. They may wall off home and work from each other completely. They may try to escape the source of pressure through illness, absenteeism, or drugs or alcohol, or by seeking temporary psychological refuge in meditation, biofeedback, or other forms of self-hypnosis. They may display increasingly rigid attitudes or appear cold and detached.

Most people, even effective managers, probably experience a near burnout at some time in their careers. A 20-year study of a group of middle managers disclosed that many of them, now in their forties and with few prospects of further promotions, were tolerating unhappy marriages, narrowing their focus to their own jobs, and showing less consideration toward other people.[3] Despite outward sociability, they were indifferent to friendships and often hostile. They had become rigid, had short fuses, and were distant from their children.

Personality tests disclosed that these managers had a greater need to do a job well for its own sake than did most of their peers and that they initially had a greater need for advancement as well (although it declined over time). They showed more motivation to dominate and lead, and less to defer to authority than other managers. While they still could do a good day's work, they could no longer invest themselves in others and in the company.

When people who feel an intense need to achieve don't reach their goals, they can become hostile to themselves and to others. They also tend to channel that hostility into more defined work tasks than before, limiting their efforts. If at times like these they do not increase their involvement in family matters, they are likely to approach burnout.

The Breeding Ground

Researchers have observed this type of exhaustion among many kinds of professionals. As the examples here indicate, it is not unusual among executives and managers, and it is more likely to occur under competitive conditions than in a stable market. Managerial jobs involve a lot of contact with other people. Often this contact is unpleasant but has to be tolerated because of the inherent demands of the job.

One problem with managing people is that such a focus creates unending stress for the manager. The manager must cope with the least capable of the employees, with the depressed, the suspicious, the rivalrous, the self-centered, and the generally unhappy. The manager must balance these conflicting personalities and create from them a motivated work group. He or she must define group purpose and organize people around it, as well as resolve conflicts, establish priorities, make decisions about other people, accept and deflect their hostility, and deal with the frustration that arises out of that continuing interaction. Managing people is the most difficult administrative task, and it has built-in frustration. That frustration can—and does—cause many managers to burn out.

Many contemporary managerial situations also provide the perfect breeding ground for cases of burnout. Today's managers face increasing time pressures with little respite. Even though benefits such as flexible working hours and longer vacations offer some relief, for the most part the modern executive's workday is long and hard. Also, as more women join the workforce, the support most men used to receive at home is lessening, and women who work get as little support as, if not less support than, the men. To many managers, the time they spend with their families is precious. It is understandable if managers feel guilty about sacrificing this part of their life to the demands of work and if they also feel frustration at being unable to do anything about it.

Adding to the stress at work is the complexity of modern organizations. The bigger and more intricate organizations become, the longer it takes to get things done. Managers trying to get ahead may well feel enormous frustration as each person or office a project passes through adds more delays and more problems to unravel before a task is finished.

Along with the increasing complexity of organizations goes an increase in the number of people that a manager has to deal with. Participative management, quality-of-work-life efforts, and matrix structures all result in a proliferation in the number of people that a manager must confront face-to-face. Building a plant, developing natural resources, or designing new products can often mean that a manager has to go through lengthy, and sometimes angry and vitriolic, interaction with community groups. Executives involved in tasks that entail controversial issues may find themselves vilified.

As companies grow, merge with other companies, or go through reorganizations, some managers feel as though they are adrift. Sacrifices they have made on behalf of the organization may well turn out to have little enduring meaning. As an organization's values change, a manager's commitment and sense of support may also shift. Another aspect of change that can add to a feeling of burnout is the threat of obsolescence. When a new position or assignment requires that managers who are already feeling taxed develop new skills, they may feel overwhelmed.

These days, change can also mean that managers have to trim jobs and demote subordinates—or maybe even discharge them. Managers whose job it is to close a plant or to go through painful labor negotiations may feel enraged at having to pay for the sins of their predecessors. Also, a fragmented marketplace can mean intense pressures on managers to come up with new products, innovative services, and novel marketing and financing schemes.

Finally, employees are making increasing demands for their rights. Managers may feel that they cannot satisfy those demands but have to respond to them nevertheless.

Prevention Is the Best Cure

Top management can take steps to keep managers out of situations in which they are likely to burn out. Of course, something as subtle as psychological exhaustion cannot be legislated against completely, but acting on the following insights can help mitigate its occurrence:

First, as with all such phenomena, recognize that burnout can, does, and will happen. The people in charge of orientation programs, management training courses, and discussions of managerial practice ought to acknowledge to employees that burnout can occur and that people's vulnerability to it is something the organization recognizes and cares about. Personnel managers should be candid with new employees about the psychological aspects of the work they are getting into, especially when that work involves intense effort of the kind I've described. The more people know, the less guilt they are likely to feel about their own perceived inadequacies when the pressures begin to mount.

Keep track of how long your subordinates are in certain jobs and rotate them out of potentially exhausting positions. Changes of pace, changes of demands, and shifts into situations that may not be so depleting enable people to replenish their energies and get new and more accurate perspectives on themselves and their roles. Change also enables people to look forward to a time when they can get out of a binding job. Long recognizing this need, the military limits the number of combat missions that air force personnel fly and the duration of tours that ground personnel must serve.

Time constraints on a job are crucial to preventing burnout. Don't allow your people to work 18 hours a day, even on critical problems. Especially don't let the same people be the rescuers of troubled situations over and over again. Understandably, managers tend to rely on their best people; but the best people are more vulnerable to becoming burned-out people. The overconscientious, in particular, need to take time off from the demands of their role and to spend that time in refreshing recreation. The military has learned this lesson, but management has not. One way to make sure people break from work is to take the whole group on a nominal business trip to a recreational site.

Some companies have set up regular formal retreats where people who work together under pressure can talk about what they are doing and how they are doing it, make long-range plans, relax and enjoy themselves, and, most important, get away from what they have to cope with every day. When managers talk together in a setting like this, they are able to make realistic assessments of the problems they are up against and their own responsibilities and limitations.

I think, for example, of the extremely conscientious engineers in many of the small electronics companies on Route 128 in the Boston area, and of those in the research triangle in North Carolina or in the Palo Alto, California, area, who have reported feeling that they simply are not developing new products fast enough. They are convinced that they aren't living up to the extremely high standards that they set for themselves. Such people need to talk together, often with a group therapist or someone else who can help them let go of some of the irrational demands they frequently make on themselves as groups and as individuals.

Make sure your organization has a systematic way of letting people know that their contributions are important. People need information that supports their positive self-image, eases their conscience, and refuels them psychologically. Many compensation and performance appraisal programs actually contribute to people's sense that their efforts will be unrecognized no matter how well they do. Organizational structures and processes that inhibit timely attacks on problems and delay competitive actions can produce much of the stress that people feel at work. If top executives fail to see that organizational factors can cause burnout, their lack of understanding may perpetuate the problem.

It is also important that top-level managers review with people their capacities, skills, and opportunities so that, armed with facts about themselves and the organization, they can make choices rather than feel trapped.

During World War II, the army discovered that it was better to send soldiers overseas in groups rather than as single replacements. It may be equally effective for managers to send groups of people from one organizational task to another rather than assemble teams of individually assigned people. When Clairol opened a new plant in California, it sent out a group of Connecticut-based managers and their spouses, who were briefed on the new assignment, the new community, and the potential stresses they might encounter. The managers discussed how they might help themselves and one another, as well as what support they needed from the organization. People who have worked together have already established mutual support systems, ways to share knowledge informally, and friendly alliances. These can prevent or ameliorate the burnout that may occur in new, difficult, or threatening tasks.

Managers should provide avenues through which people can express not only their anger but also their disappointment, helplessness, hopelessness, defeat, and depression. Some employees, such as salespeople, meet defeat every day. Others meet defeat in a crisis—when a major contract is lost, when a product expected to succeed fails, when the competition outflanks them. When people in defeat deny their angry feelings, that denial of underlying, seething anger contributes to the sense of burnout.

If top executives fail to see these problems as serious, they may worsen the situation. If a company offers only palliatives like meditation and relaxation methods—temporarily helpful though they may be—victims of burnout may become further enraged. The sufferers know that their problem has to do with the nature of the job and not their capacity to handle it.

Those managers who are exposed to attack need to talk about the hostilities they anticipate and how to cope with them. Just as sailors at sea need to anticipate and cope with storms, so executives need to learn how to cope with the public's aggression. Under attack themselves, they need to develop consensus, foster cohesion, and build trust rather than undermine themselves through counterattacks.

Another way executives can help is by defending the organization publicly against outside attacks. For example, a prominent chief executive once raised the morale of all his employees when he filed suit against a broadcast medium for making false allegations about his company's products. Another publicly took on a newspaper that had implied his organization was not trustworthy. A visible, vigorous, and powerful leader does much to counteract people's sense of helplessness.

As technology changes, you need to retrain and upgrade your managers. But some people will be unable to rise to new levels of responsibility and are likely to feel defeated if they cannot succeed in the same job. Top management needs to retrain, refresh, and reinvigorate these managers as quickly as possible by getting them to seminars, workshops, and other activities away from the organization.

As Freudenberger commented after his early observations, however, introspection is not what the burned-out person requires; rather, he or she needs intense physical activity, not further mental strain and fatigue. Retreats, seminars, and workshops therefore should be oriented toward the physical rather than the emotional. Physical exercise is helpful because it provides a healthy outlet for angry feelings and pent-up energy.

Managers who are burning out need support from others who can offer psychological sustenance. Ideally, those others should be their supervisors—people who value them as individuals and insist that they withdraw, get appropriate help, and place themselves first. In times of unmitigated strain, it is particularly important for managers to keep up personal interaction with their subordinates. To borrow from the military again, generals valued by their troops, such as George Patton and James Gavin in World War II, have made it a practice to be involved with their frontline soldiers.

Freudenberger points out that the burnout phenomenon often occurs when a leader or the leader's charisma is lost. He notes that people who join an organization still led by the founder or founding group frequently expect that person or group to be superhuman. After all, the entrepreneurs had the foresight, vision, drive, and imagination to build the organization. "As they begin to disappoint us, we bad-rap them, and the result, unless it is stopped, is psychic damage to the whole clinic," he comments.[4] The issue is the same for a clinic, a hospital, a police department, or a business.

Executives who are idealized should take time to remove their halos in public. They can do that by explaining their own struggles, disappointments, and defeats to their subordinates so that the latter can view them more accurately. They also need to help people verbalize their disappointment with the "fallen" executive hero.

When the leader leaves, through either death or transfer, when a paternalistic and successful entrepreneur sells out, or when an imaginative inventor retires, it is important for the group that remains to have the opportunity to go through a process of discussing its loss and mourning it. The group needs to conduct its own psychological wake and consider for itself how it is going to deal with the loss.

Frequently, the group will discover that, although the loss of the leader is indeed significant, it can carry on effectively and contribute to the organization's success. Failing to realize its own strengths, a group can, like the Green Bay Packers after the loss of coach Vince Lombardi, feel permanently handicapped. To my knowledge, few organizations deal effectively with the loss of a leader. Most respond with a depression or slump from which it takes years to recover. Even more crippling is the way people in the organization keep yearning and searching for a new charismatic leader to rescue them. As part of a national organization, Americans have been doing this searching ever since the death of John Kennedy.

A New Age of Self-Reliance

Fifteen years ago, executive burnout was a new phenomenon. Not so anymore. Today extreme feelings of stress are pervasive and growing worse. Reengineering, downsizing, and increased competition have multiplied pressures in the workplace. At the same time, dual-earner couples suffer time and energy famines at home. In the 1990s, it is hard to find peace anywhere.

When I wrote "When Executives Burn Out" in 1981, a chief underlying assumption was that senior management had a role to play in preventing executive burnout. My advice in the article reflected that proposition, and I suggested actions that leaders could take to prevent stress, such as supplying recreation and offering training.

This basic assumption now feels outdated. Why? Because the forces changing the world in which we work and live have also changed the relationship between the employer and the employee. As we read in the paper every day, most companies no longer expect to have long-term relationships with their employees. In turn, workers—even executives—make sure that they are not too dependent on any one job or employer. They no longer look to the employer to support them. They now look to themselves.

A psychological and practical result of these changes is that we are living in a new age of self-reliance. On a personal level, we must get feedback, advice, and moral support from family and friends. On a professional level, we each need to develop fallback positions. By *fallback,* I mean an alternative course of action if the current job fails us. In today's world, we need to worry less about the next rung up the ladder and more about the variety of possibilities available to us should the ladder disappear and we find ourselves thrown back on our own resources.

In developing our careers, most of us have thought in terms of acquiring specific competencies (such as marketing techniques, financial analysis skills, or engineering specialization). Of course, skills are necessary, but they will make little difference to us as the tools of our trade if they become outdated. A specific skill will never be an enduring source of self-reliance, because it risks losing its value in the marketplace.

To develop attractive and realistic career alternatives, we need to think more in terms of our characteristic behaviors. We must understand the behaviors that we have developed since childhood, patterns that express *who we are* instead of what we do. Whether we are naturally levelheaded, spontaneously enthusiastic, artlessly charming, or born to persevere, we take our behaviors with us into everything we do. If what you do is at the core of who you are, your stress level will go down.

In developing your fallback positions, think about what you do spontaneously. The great entertainer Myron Cohen became a comedian because he was frustrated working in the garment business but was good at telling jokes to his friends. A few years ago, we all read about a successful financier who honored his inborn musical talents by becoming a respected conductor. We hear every day about successful business-people who "chuck it all" to satisfy their deeper need to be an artist, teacher, minister, or builder of affordable housing. These people will never want to retire, because they are acting on who they truly are.

Understanding and tapping into your most characteristic behaviors will give you more security and less stress than anything else you can do. To believe otherwise is to ignore reality.

Notes

1. Herbert J. Freudenberger, "Staff Burn-Out," *Journal of Social Issues,* vol. 30, no. 1, 1974, p. 159; see also his book *Burn-Out: The Melancholy of High Achievement* (New York: Doubleday, 1980).
2. Christina Maslach, "Burn-Out," *Human Behavior,* September 1976, p. 16.
3. Douglas W. Bray, Richard J. Campbell, and Donald L. Grant, *Formative Years in Business* (New York: John Wiley, 1974).
4. Freudenberger, "Staff Burn-Out," p. 160.

Reprint 96406

Originally published in 1981, republished in July–August 1996

3
A Second Career: The Possible Dream

What manager hasn't sat at his desk on a gloomy Monday morning wondering what he was doing there and asking himself whether he could make it as the skipper of a charter boat in the Bahamas or as the operator of a ski resort in Colorado? Sometimes he dreams of becoming a lawyer, sometimes simply of writing a book. Regardless of the dream itself, however, managers need to satisfy a few conditions, this author says, before they can be sure that their choice of a second career is a wise one and not simply a flight from the routine and frustration that is common to all jobs. First managers need to understand their "ego ideals," their hidden images of how they would like to be. Then they need to determine how they prefer to behave in certain situations—whether, for instance, they prefer risk taking on their own or the security of groups. Armed with an understanding of their own visions and behavior patterns, managers are in a position to weigh their career options realistically.

Just two years after his appointment as director of marketing services, 35-year-old Tom Conant started thinking about leaving his job and enrolling in law school. He had fantasies of addressing the bench in an attempt to persuade the judge to side with his position. Tom imagined how it would feel to demolish the opposing lawyer by asking the witness penetrating questions that led inexorably to the conclusion he sought. He couldn't wait to get started.

Tom had joined the company right after business school and in 12 years there had topped one success with another. His marketing acumen, his ability to innovate, do research, and carry through new programs brought the company important new business. In other respects, too, Tom had been a model manager to his superiors and his subordinates. He was marked as a comer. Tom's initial impatience to sink his teeth into new challenges had posed some problems, but as he received new responsibilities, Tom began to relax and seemed to enjoy his work and his colleagues.

When he found himself thinking of a career in law, Tom surprised himself. He had thought that he might be wooed by competitors, but he had never expected to think of abandoning his career. Leo Burns, Tom's predecessor as manager of marketing services and his mentor, hoped to see his protégé follow him to the vice presidency. Tom knew that his resignation would shatter Leo, and that knowledge annoyed him. He didn't want to fight or disappoint Leo.

Anger at Leo slowly mounted. In his fantasy Tom tried to explain to Leo his reasons for leaving, to describe the soul-searching he had done in the last year, but Leo wouldn't listen. He pictured Leo's disappointment turning to irritation. The imaginary drama came to a climax with Leo insisting that Tom leave the company immediately. "Marketing doesn't need you!" Tom imagined Leo shouting. "Just get on with your plans and get out!"

When Tom had these fantasies, he always had second thoughts about making such a move. He had a good career ahead of him. He was a loyal company person, and the company had been good to him. His recent promotion had given him new responsibilities and a reputation in the industry. And he hadn't really been that bored for the last two years.

Yet in calmer moments Tom remembered other managers who had switched careers. An engineer he knew had left a responsible job in product development at the age of 40 to go to law school and was now a patent attorney. He boasted that it was a change he was glad he had made: "I was going to spend the rest of my life putting new faces on old products. Now I can use what I know about engineering to help people who are going to make real changes happen."

Tom reflected also about the many people in the news who were on their second, or even third, careers. California ex-governor Jerry Brown had been a Jesuit seminarian before entering politics; Henry Kissinger had been a professor before becoming a diplomat. Several business school deans had been CEOs, and university presidents have become business executives.

As always, Tom concluded his reverie with a farewell handshake; he was leaving his old friends behind. He imagined them thinking that they, too, should have undertaken second careers.

Almost everyone at some point thinks of a second career. Many people have good reasons. Tom's law school fantasy was based in part on a cool assessment of his own life and the contemporary business situation. He believed that growing consumer movements would force the marketing field to change radically in the next decade. Despite their temporary relaxation, he thought that federal, state, and local regulations controlling advertising and promotion would increase. By combining his marketing experience with a law school education, Tom reasoned he could steal a march on this trend and build a solid future for himself either as an in-house counsel or as a consultant.

As the years pass, most people—regardless of their professions or skills—find their jobs or careers less interesting, stimulating, or rewarding. By midlife, many feel the need for new and greener occupational fields. They yearn for opportunities to reassert their independence and maturity and to express the needs and use the talents of a different stage of life.

Some people feel they are no longer in the running for advancement, some that their talents and skills are not being fully used, and some that they have outgrown their jobs, companies, or disciplines. Others, feeling blocked by being in the wrong company, industry, or position, are bored. Some are in over their heads, while others had merely drifted into their jobs or chosen directions prematurely. One or a combination of these feelings can make a person hate to go to work in the morning and can trigger thoughts of a way out.

The realities of contemporary organizational life also stimulate a manager to think about a second career: the competition is stiffer every year. Even to the young manager, the accelerating pace of change makes obsolescence a threat. Rapid technological changes (which demand higher levels of education and training), more differentiated markets, and unpredictable economic circumstances all make it improbable that a manager will have a life-long career in one field or one organization.

By their middle or late 30s, managers usually know how far their careers will take them. By comparing his promotion rate to those of peers, a manager can tell if he has leveled off. If a manager's latest assignment takes him out of the organization's prescribed route to the top, the upward movement probably has ended.

Other factors behind the wish for second careers are the effects aging and growth have on people. Although an intense period of skills training, job rotation, long hours of overtime, and much traveling may have satisfied them when they were younger and just beginning their careers, managers as they get older probably find the pace exhausting and the rewards insufficiently attractive to compensate for the loss of other gratifications.

But the reasons for thinking about a second career are not always positive. Some people want to change because they are always dissatisfied with themselves; some are depressed and angry; some have anxiety about death that induces restlessness; and some have overvalued themselves and believe they are more talented or capable than they really are. Some managers can't tolerate bosses. Others think they should have been CEO a long time ago. Some are unwilling to acquire experience, while others are competing with old classmates. Some are just competing—and not as well as they'd like.

Seeking a new career for these reasons is an exercise in futility. If a manager blames the job, the boss, or the company when the source of his discontent is really himself, his second career is likely to be as disappointing as his first. Therefore a manager, before embarking on choosing a second career, must have an honest picture of himself and understand the changes he probably will go through.

Stages in Adult Development

As middle age approaches, thoughts about a second career intensify.[1] Building on the work of Sigmund Freud, psychoanalyst Erik H. Erikson has outlined three stages of adulthood: intimacy, generativity, and integrity.[2] Each stage has a psychosocial crisis and each has its task.

The first adult stage, intimacy, which lasts from about age 21 to age 35, is the most spontaneously creative period. It is an innovative and productive time. The young adult channels great energies into choosing and launching a career and, usually, into contracting a marriage and establishing a family. The third and final stage, integrity, begins at approximately age 55. Ideally, at this age a person ties together his life experience and comes to terms with his life. At work, he prepares for retirement and reflects on his career.

In between, during the stage of generativity, from about age 35 to age 55, the adult lays the foundations for the next generation. Commonly called the midlife transition, this is the time of reevaluation. At home, the children are leaving the nest and husbands and wives have to rethink their relationship to each other. At work, the drive to compete and excel is peaking, and executives pay more attention to bringing other, younger managers along.

The transition between intimacy and generativity is, according to Daniel Levinson, the time during which the adult makes his last assertion for independence.[3] Levinson calls this "the BOOM [becoming one's own man] effect." His studies of executives indicate that at about age 37, the adult throws off the guidance or protection of older mentors or managers and takes full charge of himself. Those that are able to make this last stand for independence go on to new heights. They demand more responsibility or start their own companies. Others either don't assert themselves or are rejected when they make demands. The BOOM effect is an impetus for seeking a new career.

In our culture people have opportunities to do many things. In youth they choose one and leave the others behind, but they promise themselves they'll come back to them. Fifteen years out of school, people tend to feel satiated with what they're doing—even if it is something with high status and high pay—and itch to fulfill old promises to themselves. They tend to become restless when circumstances keep them from doing so and become dismayed when they realize that they can't go back and start all over again.

When people are in this stage of life, they need to seek counsel, to talk at length about their reasons, and to listen to others' experiences and perceptions. They also need the support of others who are important to them through this difficult decision-making and transition period. Such assistance can ensure that the manager will make a sound second-career choice rather than flee impulsively from frustration or boredom. It might even result in a wise decision on the part of a promising executive to remain, with renewed enthusiasm, in his organization. A manager who thinks through the issues of a second career also readies himself to help others with the same concerns.

Who Are You?

The most critical factor for people to consider in choosing a gratifying second career is their ego ideal. It can serve as a road map. Central to a person's aspirations, the ego ideal is an idealized image of oneself in the future. It includes the goals people would like to achieve and how they would like to see themselves. At an early age, children identify with parents and other power figures, find out how to please or resist them, and learn to adapt to feeling small and helpless in comparison with them. How they do these things, as well as other unconscious factors, determines how their ego ideals develop. During childhood and adolescence, the young person incorporates rising aspirations built on academic or career achievements into the ego ideal and, as time goes on, also includes successive models, each of which has a more specialized competence.

Throughout life people strive toward their ego ideals, but no one ever achieves it. With successive accomplishments, aspirations rise. But as people feel they are progressing toward their ego ideals, their self-pictures are more rather than less positive. The closer a person gets to the ego ideal, therefore, the better he feels about himself. The greater the gap between one's ego ideal and one's current self-image, the angrier one is at oneself and the more inadequate, guilty, and depressed one feels.

When a career helps satisfy the ego ideal, life and work are rewarding and enjoyable. When a career does not help meet these self-demands, work is a curse. In short, the wish to attain the ego ideal, to like oneself, is the most powerful of motivating forces. Delivery on the promises one makes to oneself is an important aspect of choosing a new direction.

TAPPING INTO THE EGO IDEAL

Because people begin to form their ego ideals in earliest childhood, developing an accurate understanding of them is difficult. A careful review of family history and school and work experiences can go a long way in outlining the needs that are important to the ego ideal. A manager can help the process along by discussing with a listener or a friend answers to the following questions (although this exercise may strike you as off the point, there are very good reasons for carrying it out):

1. What were your father's or father substitute's values? Not what did your father say or do, but what did he stand for? What things were important to him? What was the code he lived by? And then, what were your mother's values?

2. What was the first thing you did that pleased your mother? Small children try hard to please their mothers, who are the most important figures in their lives. Every child's earliest efforts to please mother become ingrained behavior. They are, therefore, a significant part of each person's characteristic way of behaving and have an important influence on subconscious goals. Later, children try to please the father, too.

   (Sometimes, especially for women, it may be the mother's values that are more important and the activities that pleased father that weigh more heavily.)

3. Who were your childhood heroes or heroines? Did you idolize athletes, movie stars, or political figures? What kind of people do you now enjoy reading about or watching on TV? What kind of achievements do you admire?

4. Who are and were your models—relatives, teachers, scoutmasters, preachers, bosses, characters in stories? What did they say or do that made you admire them?

5. When you were able to make choices, what were they? What elective subjects did you take in high school? What major did you pursue in college? What jobs have you accepted? At first glance, these choices may seem to have been random, but they were not. And when you take a retrospective look at them, a pattern emerges.

6. What few experiences in your lifetime have been the most gratifying? Which gave you the greatest pleasure and sense of elation? The pleasure you took in the experience was really the pleasure you took in yourself. What were you doing?

7. Of all the things you've done, at which were you the most successful? What were you doing and how were you doing it?

8. What would you like your epitaph or obituary to say? What would you like to be remembered for? What would you like to leave as a memorial?

The answers to these questions will help managers sketch the outlines of their ego ideals and give them a sense of the main thrust of their lives.

If you still have some doubts about direction after you've talked these questions through, you might take a battery of psychological tests to complement the definition of your ego ideal. Many counseling psychologists provide interest, aptitude, and values inventories as well as tests of intelligence, reasoning, and other capacities. They can interpret the test results and advise you about their significance for your career choice.

How Do You Like to Act?

The next step is to determine the kinds of occupational activities that fit the way you like to behave, how you like to do your job or deal with coworkers. The point here is to determine whether you are temperamentally fit for the job you're thinking of moving to. For instance, Tom in the opening vignette had always wanted to take on new responsibilities and challenges and to act alone taking risks rather than in a group, where interdependence is important. If Tom decided to go to law school to become a consultant working on his own, he would be making a choice consistent with how he worked best. He would be choosing an environment in which he would be psychologically comfortable.

In determining how your personality will fit with a job, a listener's or friend's questions and insights will be valuable. Explore the following areas:

- How do you handle aggressive energy? Do you channel it into the organization and administration of projects? Are you reluctant to express it? For instance, do you have difficulty taking people to task or confronting colleagues or subordinates? How do you react when someone challenges your opinion?

  Channeling aggressive energy into the organization and administration of projects means that the person can comfortably take charge and can focus his achievement effort into organizational achievement rather than personal aggrandizement. A person who is reluctant to express his aggression may have difficulty speaking up at the right time or representing himself adequately or analyzing problems and discussions with other people. Difficulty in taking people to task or confronting colleagues is also a product of reluctance to express aggression and usually reflects a good deal of underlying unconscious guilt.

  A person who is unable to take people to task cannot take charge as a manager; and one who is unable to confront others cannot give colleagues or subordinates honest performance appraisals.

- How do you handle affection? Some people prefer to be independent, while others enjoy working closely with people. Do you need constant approval and encouragement or does the quality of your work satisfy you? Can you praise others or do you find it difficult to express positive feelings?

While some people enjoy the affectionate interchange and camaraderie of working closely with others, some people prefer to be independent. The latter may either deny their need for other people's praise, approval, and affection or simply feel more comfortable keeping a distance.

Many managers have great difficulty telling others when they do good work. It is as if any expression of emotion is difficult for them. For some, this is a matter of conscience: they feel like hypocrites for praising work that isn't outstanding. For others, praise may seem to invite a closer relationship with the person being praised or may violate the picture of stoic self-control they want to present.

• How do you handle dependency? Do you have trouble making decisions without your manager's OK? Do you work better when you're in charge or in a number 2 position? Do you work as well independently as on a team? Do you have difficulty asking for and using the help of others?

Although most of us fear becoming helplessly dependent on others, in organizations we are necessarily dependent on a lot of other people to get our work done. But some people can't tolerate this aspect of themselves. They need to do everything on their own. It is all right for other people to lean on them, and indeed sometimes they encourage it, but it is not all right for them to lean on other people. Such people disdain others' advice or guidance, even when seeking professional help is appropriate.

On the other hand, some people do well only when they can lean on somebody else's guidance or direction and panic when they don't have that. And while some people may work well by themselves, they may not accept other people's needs to depend on them. Such people will not be good bosses.

Listeners' or friends' special knowledge of a manager's working habits will enable them to be perceptive in questioning the manager in these areas. In addition, the manager should ask others—friends, coworkers, colleagues—to share with him their perceptions of his characteristic behavior. Sometimes they can tell the manager about working habits that he himself is not aware of. For instance, over a period of time friends might have noticed that Tom, from the opening vignette, enjoyed bearing full responsibility and risk for a project and making it work through his own expertise. This information could help Tom choose whether to join a company as in-house counsel or to become an independent consultant. A friend could point out that given his characteristic work-ing style, Tom would probably enjoy the latter better.

In some cases, of course, friends may not be very perceptive or may have their own interests at heart and not be very helpful. At times like these, managers should definitely seek professional help.

Which Way to Go?

Armed with an understanding of his ego ideal and working style, the manager is now ready to weigh options more wisely. He may choose to launch a second career or he may decide to stick with his course in the organization. Whatever his decision, his friends' support and his deeper understanding of himself and his motivation will equip him to attack his chosen career with new dedication and enthusiasm.

Second careers are evolutionary. They stem from some interest that has lain dormant or has been abandoned in favor of another occupa-tion. Asked if he had any idea of what he wanted to do when he left the chairmanship of Dain, Kalman & Quail, an investment banking firm in Minneapolis, for a new vocation, Wheelock Whitney answered, "Yes, really. I thought I'd like to pursue some other things that I cared about." Among these interests was the Johnson Institute, a center studying and treating the chemically dependent. Whitney had become deeply involved in the institute eight years earlier when his wife was undergoing treatment for alcoholism.[4]

Many turn to second careers that extend a previous occupational thrust; they may go into business for themselves in fields they already know. By searching the past for those budding interests that had no chance to flower, a manager can draw a long list of career options. At the same time, a manager can eliminate those that are no longer inter-esting or pleasurable. In choosing his second career, William Damroth said he switched from the chairmanship of Lexington Corporation because "to me the main thing was that I couldn't continue doing what I enjoy the most, which is the creative role, the intense bringing together of all factors, saying, 'It ought to look like this.' For instance, what I'm doing today is much more satisfying than the long-range planning you have to do for a company. Today's satisfaction is immediate."[5]

After eliminating undesirable options, a manager should investigate what additional training is required for each of the remaining possibili-ties and how much he can afford to invest. To pick up some careers, managers need to spend years in full-time professional or academic training; others they can approach through a course of reading, night school, or correspondence study. By seeing how the remaining options fit with how he prefers to behave and by understanding his ego ideal, a manager can usually narrow the field to one or two general directions. At this point, a manager considering a career change should again ask a friend or counselor to act as a sounding board, letting the manager talk through options and refine his ideas.

Finally, before a manager makes a choice, he should consider a number of other critical issues:

1. *Family.* Whom do you have responsibility for—a mother-in-law, an uncle, a grandfather, a handicapped sister or brother? Do these responsibilities limit your options? Do your responsibilities to your spouse and children impose geographic or financial constraints?

2. *Present job.* If a manager comes to a premature judgment or acts impulsively, he risks leaving his present job thinking that the company left much to be desired. Will your peers and boss see the move as a rejection of the company and of your work together? Feeling abandoned, they might attack you. The possibility of anger and disappointment is especially high when you and your superior have worked closely together and when you respect and admire each other. Furthermore, some people, disappointed that they failed to act when the time was right, will be jealous. They may unload on you their anger with themselves. Are you prepared for these conflicts?

   It will help you to think about what it means to lose these peers and mentors. Rather than thinking that you are being disloyal, recognize that people who prepare themselves for a second career are doing the organization as well as themselves a favor by making space for younger, talented managers looking forward to promotion.

3. *Status.* One's status in the community is directly related to one's status at work. Choosing another career may well result in changing one's status. How important is that to you? How important is it that you associate with the same people you have associated with before, that you play golf at the same clubs or take part in the same social activities? Because your spouse and children will also be affected, the family must discuss this issue together. The sacrifices may well be severe.

4. *Rebuilding.* If you're thinking of starting a new business or launching a new career, chances are that you will have to build a clientele. Rarely does a person move from one organization to another and take with him all of his accounts. For example, a lawyer told me that when he and his colleagues left a large firm to start their own, they expected their clients to follow them. Only a small fraction did, and the new firm had to build its clientele from scratch. Anyone starting his own business should expect it to take from two to five years to build a stable of customers.

5. *Freedom v. constraints.* For a mature manager in the BOOM period, the pressure to be autonomous, to do what he wants to do, to be free of commitments to somebody else, is very high. Therefore, in choosing an activity or direction, it is important to choose, insofar as you can, something that allows you maximum freedom to come and go, to do as you wish, while meeting the formal obligations of the role. As William Damroth comments: "My time is my own. I can lie on my back for two hours if I want. Instead of saying, 'This is what I want' and moving toward it, I've said 'This is what I don't like,' and I've eliminated it. I've cut away all the things that make life unhappy for me. I don't have any tension headaches in the mornings."[6]

But one doesn't always achieve freedom so easily. As we go through life we aspire to many things—promotions, new roles, different experiences. And we often ask ourselves, "Who am I to want to do that? What right do I have to seek that goal?" Self-critical feelings often prevent us from moving toward aspirations that we have every right to work toward and achieve.

The issue becomes particularly important with respect to a second career. Because a mature manager recognizes, if he hasn't before, that he has every right to pursue anything he wants to, now is the time to act. Anyone is eligible for any aspiration. One may not achieve it, but one has as much right as anybody else to want it and try for it.

6. *Year-long depression.* I have never seen a person make a significant career shift without experiencing a year-long depression. I don't mean that people are down in the dumps for a year but that they feel loss, ambivalence, and fear that things may not work out. Caught in an ambiguous situation in which they are not yet rooted, they feel detached from their stable routines.

The longer the manager has been with an organization, the more likely he has come to depend on it; the closer his relationships have been with his colleagues, the greater will be the sense of loss. The more his family has been tied to the organization, the more profound these feelings are likely to be.

7. *Talk.* All change is loss and all loss requires mourning.[7] Even when promoted, one loses the support of colleagues, friends, and known ways of doing things. To dissipate the inevitable sorrow, you have to turn it into words. To detach yourself from old ties and give up old habits, you have to talk about the experience. Feeling that they have to be heroic, some managers, men particularly, either deny that they are having such experiences or grit their teeth and try to plow through them. That way of acting doesn't deal with the depression; it only buries it and makes one vulnerable to physiological symptoms and overreactions when traumas occur.

It is important to have somebody to talk to and to be able to talk to that person freely. But even with the most careful and sensitive support from spouse and friends, you may get sidetracked, spin your wheels and get stuck in the mire. If after such talk you are no clearer about your choice, it may be time to consult a professional. The issues and feelings any careful self-appraisal touches on are often too complex to examine or discuss without professional help.

8. *Joint experiences.* Husbands' and wives' careers often separate them. When one member of the marriage makes a career change, new problems having to do with adult development emerge. Early in a marriage the spouses go in different directions, the husband usually to earn a livelihood and the wife usually to bear children. After her childrearing is done, the wife may return to work, but chances are nevertheless that the two spouses will still go in different occupational directions. Their only common interest tends to be the children or family problems.

Usually by the time a person has reached midcareer, the children are out on their own or close to it. The spouses now have to talk to each other. But if they have gone in different directions, they may have trouble communicating. A second career can help spouses reunite. One couple, for example, became interested in antiques. Together they went to antique shows and searched for old glass.

When they gave up their old careers, they decided to run an antique store together. What was originally a shared hobby gave the couple financial security while they worked together.

Sometimes a new career threatens an old relationship. One manager was successful and widely respected in his organization. Although unequal to him in status or earning power, his wife also had professional training. When they decided to have children, she left her job to rear them. During those years, he was a supportive helpmate. When she was able, she went to law school and subsequently entered a prestigious law firm. Her status and income now exceed her husband's. He has taken a backseat to her and, with some feelings of embarrassment, carries on some of the household and family maintenance activities that she formerly handled. He speaks of his new situation with mingled pride and shame and is now considering a second career himself.

9. *Open options.* Even if you have exercised great care in choosing a second career, the change won't necessarily work out. Economic vagaries as well as factors that you couldn't foresee may cut your second career short. If you left your old job on a positive note, however, it may be possible to get it back. Many organizations recognize that a manager who has tested himself elsewhere and wants to return is likely to be an even better and more highly motivated employee.

Notes

1. See my article, "On Being a Middle-Aged Manager," HBR July–August 1969, p. 57.

2. Erik H. Erikson, *Childhood and Society,* 2d ed. (New York: Norton, 1963).

3. Daniel Levinson, Charlotte N. Darrow, Edward B. Klein, Maria H. Levinson, and Braxton McKee, *The Seasons of a Man's Life* (New York: Alfred A. Knopf, 1978).

4. See "Don't Call It Early Retirement," HBR interview with Wheelock Whitney and William G. Damroth, HBR September–October 1975, p. 103.

5. Ibid, p. 113.

6. Ibid, p. 118.

7. See my article, "Easing the Pain of Personal Loss," HBR September–October 1972, p. 80.

Reprint 88307

Originally published in May–June 1983.

4
What Killed Bob Lyons?

Bob Lyons serves as an extreme example of the conflicting forces in all of us. Successful, hard-working, aggressive, he drives himself relentlessly. What happens when he can no longer balance the demands of internal forces with those of external reality? What can we learn from his tragedy about the problems, pressures, and anxieties with which we must deal?

The case and the extensive analysis that follows were originally published in HBR in 1963. A penetrating study of some of the possible causes of self-destructive behavior, the article provides insight into an area of human psychology that continues to be of major concern to HBR readers. In his retrospective commentary, the author explains why the article has endured. He argues for the validity of Freudian psychoanalytic theory and briefly discusses six major trends in psychoanalysis that provide a contemporary perspective.

Those who knew Bob Lyons thought extremely well of him. He was a highly successful executive who held an important position in a large company. As his superiors saw him, he was aggressive, with a knack for getting things done through other people. He worked hard and set a vigorous pace. He drove himself relentlessly. In less than 10 years with his company, he had moved through several positions of responsibility.

Lyons had always been a good athlete. He was proud of his skill in swimming, hunting, golf, and tennis. In his college days he had lettered in football and baseball. On weekends he preferred to undertake rebuilding and repairing projects around the house or to hunt, interspersing other sports for a change of pace. He was usually engaged, it seemed, in hard physical work.

His life was not all work, however. He was active in his church and in the Boy Scouts. His wife delighted in entertaining and in being with other people, so their social life was a round of many parties and social activities. They shared much of their life with their three children.

Early in the spring of his ninth year with the company, Bob Lyons spoke with the vice president to whom he reported. "Things are a little quiet around here," he said. "Most of the big projects are over. The new building is finished, and we have a lot of things on the ball that four years ago were all fouled up. I don't like this idea of just riding a desk and looking out the window. I like action."

About a month later, Lyons was assigned additional responsibilities. He rushed into them with his usual vigor. Once again he seemed buoyant and cheerful. After six months on the assignment, Lyons had the project rolling smoothly. Again he spoke to his vice president, reporting that he was out of projects. The vice president, pleased with Lyons's performance, told him that he had earned the right to do a little dreaming and planning; and, furthermore, dreaming and planning were a necessary part of the position he now held, toward which he had aspired for so long. Bob Lyons listened as his boss spoke, but it was plain to the vice president that the answer did not satisfy him.

About three months after this meeting, the vice president began to notice that replies to his memos and inquiries were not coming back from Lyons with their usual rapidity. In addition, he noticed that Lyons was beginning to put things off, a most unusual behavior pattern for him. He observed that Lyons became easily angered and disturbed over minor difficulties, which previously had not irritated him at all.

Bob Lyons then became involved in a conflict with two other executives over a policy issue. Such conflicts were not unusual in the organization since, inevitably, there were varying points of view on many issues. The conflict was not personal, but it did require intervention from higher management before a solution could be reached. In the process of resolving the conflict, Lyons's point of view prevailed on some questions but not on others.

A few weeks after this conflict had been resolved, Lyons went to the vice president's office. He wanted to have a long private talk, he said. His first words were, "I'm losing my grip. The old steam is gone. I've had diarrhea for four weeks and several times in the past three weeks I've lost my breakfast. I'm worried and yet I don't know what about. I feel that some people have lost confidence in me."

He talked with his boss for an hour and a half. The vice president recounted his achievements in the company to reassure him. He then asked if Lyons thought he should see a doctor. Lyons agreed that he should and, in the presence of the vice president, called his family doctor for an appointment. By this time the vice president was very much concerned. He called Mrs. Lyons and arranged to meet her for lunch the next day. She reported that, in addition to his other symptoms, her husband had difficulty sleeping. She was relieved that the vice president had called her because she was beginning to become worried and had herself planned to call the vice president. Both were now alarmed. They decided that they should get Lyons into a hospital rather than wait for the doctor's appointment that was still a week off.

The next day Lyons was taken to the hospital. Meanwhile, with Mrs. Lyons's permission, the vice president reported to the family doctor Lyons's recent job behavior and the nature of their conversations. When the vice president had finished, the doctor concluded, "All he needs is a good rest. We don't want to tell him that it may be mental or nervous." The vice president replied that he didn't know what the cause was, but he knew Bob Lyons needed help quickly.

During five days in the hospital, Lyons was subjected to extensive laboratory tests. The vice president visited him daily. He seemed to welcome the rest and the sedation at night. He said he was eating and sleeping much better. He talked about company problems, though he did not speak spontaneously without encouragement. While Lyons was out of the room, another executive who shared his hospital room confided to the vice president that he was worried about Lyons. "He seems to be so morose and depressed that I'm afraid he's losing his mind," the executive said.

By this time the president of the company, who had been kept informed, was also becoming concerned. He had talked to a psychiatrist and planned to talk to Lyons about psychiatric treatment if his doctor did not suggest it. Meanwhile, Lyons was discharged from the hospital as being without physical illness, and his doctor recommended a vacation. Lyons remained at home for several days where he was again visited by the vice president. He and his wife took a trip to visit friends. He was then ready to come back to work, but the president suggested that he take another week off. The president also suggested that they visit together when Lyons returned.

A few days later, the president phoned the Lyonses' home. Mrs. Lyons could not find him to answer the telephone. After 15 minutes she still had not found him and called the vice president about her concern. By the time the vice president arrived at the Lyonses' home, the police were already there. Bob Lyons had committed suicide.

Why Did It Happen?

This tragic story is not unusual. Probably no other single emotional problem is as disturbing to those who must live with it as is suicide. No doubt Bob Lyons's colleagues and superiors suffered almost as much anguish as his family did. The president and vice president were concerned long afterward. They wondered if, despite their conscientious efforts, they had in some way been at fault or if they could have prevented it. Neither his family nor his colleagues could understand why it happened. Why should a successful man in the prime of his life, like Lyons, destroy himself?

Lyons's problem may have been extreme, but similar problems are not rare in business and industry. Executives, managers, supervisors, industrial physicians, and—to a lesser extent—all employees frequently must cope with emotional problems on the job. Many problems are of lesser proportion than Lyons's was, but all have four factors in common:

- They are painful both for the person who suffers from them and for those who must deal with that person.
- They are usually destructive to both the sufferer and the organization.
- The origins of the problem are almost always more complex than either party realizes; and only infrequently are even the precipitating events clear.
- Rarely does the person responsible for dealing with the on-the-job problem know what he or she should do about it.

As a result, few businesses have ways of dealing with these matters even reasonably well, and management actions tend to range from abrupt firing to hostile discipline to, in some instances, procrastination that goes on for years. Often management makes a vacillating series of efforts, accompanied by feelings of guilt, failure, and anger on the part of those who must make the managerial decisions. Emotional problems, then, are contagious. The disturbance suffered by one person affects the emotions of others.

WAS IT HEREDITARY?

How can we understand what happened to Bob Lyons and the ways his problem relates to problems with which all of us must deal? The customary commonsense reasons fail us. He had no serious illness. He did not fail in his business activity. There was no indication of difficulty in his family life. The course of the story told by the vice president is too consistent to attribute his death to an accident or to chance. What then was responsible?

Heredity? Can we say he inherited a tendency to suicide? People inherit certain capacities and traits, but these are essentially physiological. They inherit eye color, nose size, and other physical features. In addition, they inherit certain sensory and motor capacities. That is, they will be able to see, hear, or feel physical stimuli—color, sound, warmth—more or less keenly. Newborn infants in a hospital nursery vary widely in their response to such stimuli. Some are calm and placid; an attendant can drop a metal tray with a clang, but these children continue to sleep. Others, however, are startled and awake crying.

The reasons for these differences in reaction are obscure. We have some clues from experiments with white rats. When pregnant rats are placed in crowded cages or in other situations where they experience stress, this stress apparently produces biochemical imbalances in the mothers that affect the rat fetuses. When the baby rats are born, they have greater anxiety and greater difficulty in adapting to the external world than rats whose mothers were not subjected to such stress. Among human beings, the mother's diet, the illnesses she has during pregnancy, and her general physical condition affect the human fetus.

SOMETHING PHYSICAL?

Apparently people also inherit the capacity to coordinate their muscles with greater or lesser efficiency. A person who inherits excellent coordination potential and develops it may ultimately become a good athlete or a good musician. One who inherits a better than usual capacity for abstracting sights and sounds may have the makings of an artist. People do not inherit athletic or artistic skill, but some inherit such a high level of sensitivity and physiological harmony that they seem to have a "natural bent" toward certain talents.

Some apparently are born with greater general intelligence; therefore, they have the potential for dealing with their environment with better reasoning power and more effective judgment. Others have more specialized capacities: the ability to abstract ideas readily, the ability to remember well, and so on. Such differences, which in some instances appear at birth, bring about different kinds of interactions with the environment. The irritable infant will have quite a different relationship with his or her mother than will the placid child. The child who walks and talks early comes into contact sooner with a wider range of experiences than does another child in the same general environment, in whom these skills develop later.

Heredity, then, to a large extent determines what a person will be—short or tall, intelligent or unintelligent, and with different thresholds of the various senses. People differ in the combination of endowments that they have and in the degree to which those endowments enable them to cope with life's stresses.

Hereditary factors predispose people to behave in gross, or general, ways but have little direct effect on specific behavior. Because of the high level of development of the frontal lobes of the brain, people are capable of both abstract and reflective thinking and are also capable of a wide range of emotions, particularly feelings about themselves in relation to other people. These capacities for thought and feeling make human beings extremely responsive to many nuances of environmental stimulation and also make it possible for them to initiate a wide range of actions in keeping with their thoughts and feelings, as well as to respond to their environment, particularly to others in it.

FAMILY INFLUENCE?

Another environmental factor that has an important influence on behavior is the extremely long period, particularly in Western cultures, during which human children depend on their parents. The intimacy of these relationships and the many social pressures that are transmitted through the parents to the children make family influences extremely important in guiding and controlling behavior. The extended period of dependency also presents a psychological problem because each person must then resolve the conflict between the wish to retain the pleasures of dependency and the desire to become an independent adult.

No one ever completely gives up the former or completely attains the latter.

Individuals seek some way of being interdependent with others that enables them to depend on others without losing their pride—because others in turn depend on them. Each person has dependency needs to varying degrees, the extent depending on how well each one has resolved this problem. Some who have not resolved it well will always be more dependent than others. Some have resolved it reasonably well and can accept whatever dependency needs they have. Some have rejected or denied such needs and will have nothing to do with situations in which they might have to depend on others.

So, too, different companies will require different degrees of dependency in their employees. People who remain in a stable public utility company for a long time will be more dependent on their company for their security than will itinerant salespeople who sell magazines on commission. The fact that such a range of possibilities is available for fulfilling such needs at work is one of the health-giving aspects of work in business organizations.

Something Inside Him

Thus, we cannot very well say that Bob Lyons committed suicide because of heredity. We might be able to say hereditary factors, interacting with environmental factors, led to his death; but in our present state of knowledge it would be extremely difficult to demonstrate a hereditary predisposition that contributed to his self-destruction. Of necessity, we must call on more purely psychological factors for an explanation. In a way, when people in despair over why someone like Bob Lyons would kill himself cry out, "There must have been something odd inside of him that drove him into doing it," they are partially right. Inside all of us are many emotional drives that seem odd when we do not understand them.

To try to understand these drives, let us return for a moment to the first paragraph of his superiors' description of Lyons. There we find these phrases: "highly successful," "aggressive," "a knack for getting things done through other people," "worked hard," "set a vigorous pace," and "drove himself relentlessly." These phrases speak of drive or energy. The subsequent two paragraphs describe other ways in which he discharged his energy. Some of these ways were highly useful to himself, his company, his family, and his friends. Others had a destructive potential: "He drove himself relentlessly." In fact, his difficulties seemed to begin when he could no longer drive himself on his job.

WARRING DRIVES

The theories of Sigmund Freud help us understand the importance of such drives. According to Freud, two psychological drives constantly operate in the personality. One is a *constructive drive* and the other a *destructive drive.* Just as there are always processes of growth and destruction in all biological matter, anabolism and catabolism, so there are similar processes in the personality. These drives constitute the basic, primitive energy sources for the personality.

The constructive drive (sometimes referred to as the *libido*) is the source of feelings of love, creativity, and psychological growth. The destructive drive gives rise to feelings of anger and hostility to others. The twin forces are variously referred to as love and hate, or in terms of Greek mythology as Eros and Thanatos, or sex and aggression. (Used in this way, both of the terms *sex* and *aggression* have a far broader meaning than they do in ordinary usage.)

A major psychological task for every human being is to fuse these drives so the constructive drive tempers, guides, and controls the destructive drive; the energy from both sources may thus be used to further individual self-interests and those of society. If we speak of the destructive drive as the aggressive drive (recognizing that we are using the word *aggressive* according to its dictionary meaning and not as synonymous with assertion as in ordinary usage), we can say that it is far better for a person to use the aggressive drive—tempered by larger amounts of the constructive drive—in the pursuit of a career, the creation of a family, and in business competition than in destroying others as might be the case if the drives were not adequately fused.

Perhaps an analogy will help. Think of an automobile engine. A mixture of gasoline and oxygen serves as the energy source. If there is too much gasoline, the engine will flood, and if there is too much oxygen, it will sputter and die. With the right blend or fusion of fuel—and particularly with considerably more gasoline than oxygen, which is then channeled through a mechanical structure—the automobile engine can serve a useful purpose.

CHANNELING THE DRIVES

In Bob Lyons's case we saw that his constructive and aggressive drives, and usually more of the former than the latter, were well fused and channeled into his work, his relationships with his family, and community service. But in some areas his destructive drive was dominant, for he drove himself, as the vice president put it, "relentlessly."

The two drives are included in a part of the personality (a set of psychological, not physical, functions) to which Freud gave the name *id,* the Latin neuter for "it." In addition to the two basic drives, the id also includes many memories and experiences that the person can no longer recall.

The brain acts like a vast tape recorder. Theoretically, people should be able to recall all of the experiences and feelings about those experiences they have had. We know that under hypnosis, in psychoanalysis, and under the influence of some drugs, people can recall many experiences although unable to do so before, no matter how hard they tried. Many of these memories, feelings, and impulses (impulses are derivatives of drives) are *repressed* or buried in the id. But they are still "alive" because they would be expressed, as we shall see later, if there were not adequate controls. For the id cares little about restraint; it operates on the pleasure principle: "I want what I want when I want it."

Repression, incidentally, is the process of "forgetting" or of making unconscious certain kinds of experiences and information that may be too troublesome or painful to handle on a conscious level. Here is how repression may have worked in Bob Lyons's case:

To judge from his behavior, he may have learned in his childhood that the only way to obtain love from his parents was by good performance. If high performance was the price of love, Lyons may well have resented his parents' attitude. But since such a conscious feeling of anger toward his parents would have been painful to live with, it was repressed. Lyons was no longer aware of his anger toward them, but it remained with him. The id, being unconscious, has no sense of time; it is inconsistent, contradictory, and not amenable to logic or persuasion. Thus, the early experiences that caused Bob Lyons's feelings of resentment were still "alive" and painful in his id.

In speaking of the drives, I have said that psychological growth and survival require more of the constructive drive, implying that individuals differ in the amount of drive energy they have. We don't know how these differences come about, nor do we have any satisfactory way of specifying amount other than grossly and comparatively. We do know, however, that warm, affectionate relationships, especially those between mother and child, give added strength to the constructive drive, while those in which the child experiences severe frustration and hostility from others stimulate more aggression in the child. In general, the same is true of adults: the relationships and experiences that provide affection and gratification bring out the good side of people, while those that precipitate frustration and anger bring out the bad side.

Something Outside Him

Not only did Bob Lyons (as do all of us) have the major psychological task of balancing or fusing his constructive and aggressive drives, but he also had to discharge these drives in socially acceptable ways only. It might have been permissible in more primitive times to hit a man on the head and take his wife, but it is no longer so. There are stringent cultural controls on how love and aggression may be expressed.

These controls on how we may express our basic drives vary from culture to culture, even from one social class to another; but they are transmitted through parents and other authority figures to children. Early in a child's development, the parents control and direct his or her behavior. They permit some forms but prohibit others. As children grow older, they incorporate into their own personalities what their parents have taught them. Children will incorporate these rules and values most effectively if they feel an affectionate bond with the parents and want to be like them. This is one of the reasons the parent-child relationship is so important and why it should be one that enables the child to feel happy and secure.

Various values and rules can be "pounded into" children, but these tend not to be genuinely theirs. They live by them only as long as external pressures require them to and abandon them when the external pressures diminish. Some parents who try to force piety and goodness into their children are dismayed to find them neither pious nor good when they grow up.

STILL, SMALL VOICE

When children develop a conscience, they become self-governing. In Freudian terms, they develop a *superego*, which is made up of four parts:

(1) the values of the culture as transmitted through parents, teachers, friends, scout leaders, ministers, and so on; (2) rules, prohibitions, and taboos; (3) an ego ideal—the image of ourselves at our future best that we never fully attain and as a result of which we are perennially discontented with ourselves; and (4) a police-judging or self-critical function.

Some theorists separate the superego and the conscience. They limit the superego to the values and the ego ideal (parts 1 and 3 cited), and refer to the rules (part 2) and the self-critical function (part 4) as the conscience. While that distinction is important scientifically, for our purposes we can ignore it. We will consider the conscience to be a part of the superego and include all four factors in the superego, as mentioned.

The superego begins to develop in the child the first time the words "no" or "don't" enter his or her small world. Its general form tends to be established by the time the child enters elementary school, although it becomes further refined and expanded as the person grows up. Some features of the superego, developed early in life, are not conscious. The person is no longer aware of why he or she must live by certain rules and values but knows only that if these are not obeyed, he or she feels uncomfortable or experiences anxiety. Some children, for example, feel that they must be the best in their class. They may not know why; but if they are not always successful, they feel they are no good.

CONSCIENCE AND CULTURE

Because the superego is acquired from the culture in which a person lives (principally through the parents and later by incorporating the values, rules, and ideals of others he or she respects), it is reinforced by the culture. The superego may keep a person from stealing, for example, but there are also social penalties for stealing. Cultural changes may, in turn, bring about some changes in the superego, particularly in those aspects of the superego that are conscious. Thus, every older generation contends that every younger generation is going to the dogs. While certain basic values and rules endure, others change with time. This is also why many parents are so concerned about where the family lives and about the beliefs and attitudes of their children's teachers and friends.

Among the directions that the superego provides are those which have to do with how the constructive and aggressive drives may be directed, how a person may love and hate (and under what circumstances), and what kind of an adult he or she should be. For example, a man may love his parents but in a way different from the way he loves his wife. He may not, in Western cultures, love another woman as he loves his wife. In Italy and Spain he may express affection to other men by embracing them but not in the United States. He may express his anger verbally but not in physical attack. He may direct some of his aggressive drive into work, sports, and community activities but not comfortably into those areas that in his culture are commonly regarded as feminine.

There are many variations among families and subcultures that become part of the superegos of people in those groups. Middle-class American families heavily emphasize achievement, cleanliness, good manners, hard work, and the avoidance of open expressions of hostility. Lower-class families, particularly those at the lowest socioeconomic levels, are not particularly concerned about these values. Some fundamentalist religious groups prohibit drinking and dancing. Some groups teach their children they are sinful by nature, others that almost anything their children want to do is acceptable.

'KNOW THEN THYSELF'

People's self-images are related to their superegos. One measure of self-evaluation is the disparity between their ego ideals and how they perceive themselves at present. When people are depreciated by others who are important to them, this reinforces the critical aspects of the superego and lowers self-esteem. When self-esteem is enhanced, however, this counteracts the criticism of the superego and neutralizes some of the aggressive drive, thus stimulating individuals to an expanded, more confident view of themselves and their capacities.

It has been said that no wound is as painful as that inflicted by the superego. When people behave in ways not in keeping with the values and rules they have made a part of themselves or when, in their judgment, they fall too short of their ego ideals, the superego induces a feeling of guilt. For most of us guilt feelings are so strong and so painful that we try to make up for violations of the superego by some form of atonement. The religious concept of penance is a recognition of this phenomenon. Restitution is another way to relieve guilt feelings. It is not unusual to see newspaper articles about people who have anonymously sent money to the government because they cheated on their taxes years before. Government officials speak of this as "conscience money."

Because the development of the superego begins early and children are not in a position to judge rationally the relative importance of some of the rules they are taught, it is easy for them to learn to judge themselves more harshly than they should. With their limited capacity to reason, children may blame themselves for events they had nothing to do with. For example, suppose a two-year-old child is severely hurt in a fall. His four-year-old brother, who must inevitably have some feelings of hostility and rivalry toward the younger child, may come to feel he is responsible. As a matter of fact, he had nothing to do with the fall, but for a small child the wish is often tantamount to the act. To wish the younger child to be destroyed may be the same to a four-year-old as actually having pushed him. He may then harbor irrational guilt feelings for many years thereafter, completely unaware that he has such feelings or how they came about.

Since there is love and hate in every relationship, children have considerable hostility toward, as well as affection for, their parents. Usually young children do not understand that their hostile feelings are not "bad" and that parents will not be destroyed merely because their children have such feelings. As a result, most of us carry a considerable load of irrational guilt feelings. One of the major tasks in some forms of psychological treatment for people who are emotionally disturbed is to make such irrational unconscious feelings conscious so that their irrationality may be recognized, and they will no longer plague the person.

THE BALANCE WHEEL

The superego, then, becomes a built-in governor, as it were. It is the internalized civilizing agent. Without it, there would be no continuing self-guide to behavior. The superego is an automatic protective device. Because of it some issues are never raised; we never even ask, "Should I or should I not steal?" As a guide to behavior it makes for stability and consistency of performance.

If, however, the values and rules that the child is taught are inconsistent, then the superego will be inconsistent. If there are too many, too strict rules, then the superego becomes a harsh taskmaster, either constricting too narrowly the way a person can behave or burdening him or her excessively with feelings of guilt and demanding constant atone-ment. But even without punishment or strict rules, a tyrannical super-ego can develop—if performance is the basis for obtaining love and if there are unrealistic expectations of extremely high performance. In such cases, people's behavior tends to have a driven quality. They feel that there is so much they should do or must do as contrasted with so much they would enjoy doing. They feel uncomfortable unless con-stantly doing what they feel they should—but without knowing exactly why. Lyons, for example, not only drove himself relentlessly but also usually had to be working hard.

We have seen so far that the constructive and aggressive drives, which continuously seek discharge, are major motivating forces in the personality. The superego, with its capacity to induce guilt feelings, not only defines acceptable ways in which the drives may be discharged but also serves as a motivating force.

HOME AND JOB

Not everything we do, of course, is completely influenced by our emo-tional drives. Environment also plays a part and should be considered in our attempt to understand Bob Lyons's suicide. For, in addition to the task of balancing or fusing our drives in keeping with the strictures of the superego, we do have to deal with our external environment. At times, this environment is a source of affection, support, and security. An infant in a mother's arms, a woman in a happy marriage, a man enjoying himself among his friends, an individual building a business, a minister serving a congregation—all draw emotional nourishment from the environment. Such nourishment strengthens the construc-tive forces of the personality.

Looked at closely, *needs for status, recognition, and esteem are essentially needs for love and affection.* Each person, no matter how old or jaded, wants to be held in esteem by some others. Few can survive long with-out giving and receiving love, though often these expressions are thor-oughly disguised, even from the self. Status needs have to do with the constructive forces of the personality as I have described them here. One who seeks recognition or status symbols simply searches for con-crete indications that some others do or will hold him or her in esteem. One way to describe status needs is to say that the person needs infusions of love and of gratification to foster his or her own strength by supporting his or her self-image.

However, the environment may also stimulate aggression: anger and jealousy, exploitation, competition for various advantages, economic reverses, wars, and so on. Every person has to deal with the realities of the environment—whether with the necessities of earning a living, the frustration of an unsolved problem, the achievement of personal goals, the development of satisfying relationships with other people, or something else. We saw that Lyons was actively involved with all of these things in his environment.

Ego and Reality

Now I have spoken of three sets of forces—id drives, the superego, and the environment—each interacting with the others, which must be kept in sufficient balance or equilibrium so that a person can function effectively. Some mechanism is required to do the balancing task, to serve as the executive part of the personality. Such a component of personality must fuse the drives, control their discharge in keeping with the conditions set by the superego, and act on the environment. Freud gave the name *ego* to this set of psychological functions. We tend to speak of the ego as a thing; actually, the term is merely a short way of describing *the organized executive functions of the personality, those functions that have to do with self-control and with testing reality.*

The ego includes such mental functions as recall, perception, judgment, attention, and conceptual or abstract thinking—those aspects of the personality that enable the individual to receive, organize, interpret, and act on stimuli or psychological and physiological data. The ego develops (not as well in those who are mentally retarded) as the person grows. Like a computer, the ego acquires and stores information in the form of memory images, particularly information and experiences that previously have led to successful solution of problems. When an impulse arises from one of the drives, the ego contains the impulse until, in effect, it has checked with the superego and determined the consequences of acting on the impulse.

The impulse may have to be fully contained or modified to meet both the conditions of the superego and the demands of the environment. The ego presumably checks its memory images to find acceptable ways of refining and discharging the impulse. When the ego can do this well, we speak of a strong ego or of psychological maturity. When it cannot do so adequately, we say a person does not have adequate ego strength or that he or she is immature. *The ego acts on the basis of what is called the reality principle:* "What are the long-run consequences of this behavior?"

The process of checking the memory images and organizing a response is what we know as thinking. Thinking is trial action or a "dry run," as it were. Sometimes it goes on consciously, but much of the time it is an unconscious process. Thinking delays impulses until they can be discharged in the most satisfactory way the person knows how. When a person acts impulsively in minor ways, for instance, in being inconsiderate of another person, we commonly speak of such behavior as "thoughtless."

The ego, operating on the reality principle and obeying the superego, must contain, refine, or redirect id impulses so that the integrity of the personality is preserved. The ego is constantly concerned with the costs and consequences of any action. In other words, the ego is concerned with psychological economy.

BELEAGUERED EGO

This task puts the ego in a difficult position. This system of psychological functions is always a buffer between the other systems, the id and the superego, and also between them and the forces of the environment. The ego, then, is always under pressure. To carry on its integrating function well requires considerable strength. Strength comes from several sources: the basic inherited capacities, experiences of love and gratification that enhance the constructive forces, the development of skills and abilities that help it master the environment, and the physical health of the person. The ego may be weakened through physical injury or illness—a brain tumor, a debilitating sickness—or by having to devote too much of its energy to repressing or otherwise coping with severe multiple or chronic emotional pressures.

The ego cannot deal with all of the stimuli that impinge on it. It is constantly being bombarded with all kinds of data and would be swamped if it tried to deal with all of the information it had in the form of both past and present experiences. It must be selective. Some data are therefore passed directly on to the id. The ego is never consciously aware of them. Furthermore, it has not been able to successfully resolve all of its psychological problems, some of which are extremely painful. With these it acts on the thesis, "If you can't lick it, forget it." These problems are repressed or "pushed down" into the id. The little boy who erroneously thought he hurt his brother, then repressed his guilt feelings, is a case in point.

Perhaps some other examples will help us to understand these processes better:

- Suppose someone walking along the street sees a new car parked at the curb. He has an impulse to take the car and, acting on the impulse, drives it off. We say he acted impulsively, by which we mean he was governed by an impulse from the id and not by rational considerations. To put it another way, we might say that the ego was weak, that it did not anticipate the consequences of the act and control the impulse. The price paid for acting on the impulse, perhaps a jail term, is high for what little momentary pleasure might have been gained. We say such a person is immature, meaning that his or her ego is not sufficiently developed to act in a wiser and less costly way.

- A store manager may also be said not to have good judgment if she bought items without thinking through their marketing possibilities or merely because she liked the salesperson. This is another form of impulsiveness or immaturity. Marketers count on the irrational impulsiveness in all of us by creating in supermarkets such a vast array of stimuli to our desires for pleasure that the ego does not function quite as well as it might. Impulse buying results—unless the ego is bolstered by additional support in the form of a shopping list and a budget.

- Here is a more personal example. If you observe young children, you see their lives are extremely active. They have many pleasant moments and some painful ones. They remember experiences from day to day and recall exciting events like a trip to the zoo with great relish. Now try to remember your own early childhood experiences, especially those that occurred before you were four or five. Probably you will be able to recall few in detail, if you can recall any at all. Many other experiences of childhood, adolescence, and even adulthood are beyond voluntary recall. Yet under hypnosis they can be recalled. This information, much of it not immediately necessary to solve today's problems, is stored in the id.

  Memory traces of some of these experiences, which might help us solve problems, are stored in the ego, though even they are usually not conscious. A person may be surprised to arrive home, having driven from work while preoccupied with a problem, without ever having noticed the turns, stoplights, or other cars. Obviously, that person used many cues and did many specific things to get home safely but did so without being aware of his or her actions.

• A final example illustrates how the ego deals with impulses from the id. Suppose an attractive secretary comes to work in a new dress whose lines are calculated to stimulate the interest of men—in short, to stimulate the sexual impulse. When this impulse reaches the ego of one of the men in the office, the ego, acting within limits set by the superego ("Look, but don't touch") and based on its judgment of the consequences of venting the impulse ("You'll destroy your reputation"), will control and refine the impulse. The man may then comment, "That's a pretty dress"—a highly attenuated derivative of the original impulse. Another man with a more rigid superego might never notice the dress. His superego would protect him by automatically prohibiting the ego from being sensitive to such a stimulus.

Ego's Assistants

If the ego has the job of first balancing the forces from the id, the superego, and the environment, and then of mediating and synchronizing them into a system that operates relatively smoothly, it requires the assistance of two kinds of psychological devices to make its work possible. Thus:

1. It needs *anxiety* to serve as an alarm system to alert it to possible dangers to its equilibrium.
2. It must have *defense mechanisms* that can be called into play, triggered by the alarm system; these will help it either to fend off the possible threats or to counteract them.

ANXIETY'S PURPOSE

We are conscious of the alarm-triggering system called anxiety whenever we are afraid of something. It is a feeling of unease or tension. But a much more subtle and complex phenomenon of anxiety operates spontaneously and unconsciously whenever the ego is threatened. Being unaware of its operation, we may not know consciously why we are restless, tense, or upset. Bob Lyons, we recall, was worried but did not know why. We have all experienced his anxiety. A feeling of tension and restlessness that one person picks up from another is very common. Sensing that the other person is upset makes us feel uneasy for reasons which are not very clear to us. We do not consciously decide that we are threatened, but we feel we "can't relax," that we must be on guard.

Perhaps the work of unconscious anxiety may be likened to a gyroscope on a ship or an airplane. The gyroscope must sense the imbalance of the ship or plane as a result of waves, currents, or storms. It must then set into motion counteracting forces to regain the vehicle's balance. This analogy highlights something else for us. *There is no state of placid emotional stability, just as there is never a smooth ocean or an atmosphere devoid of air currents. There is no peace of mind short of the grave. Everyone is always engaged in maintaining psychological equilibrium.* Even when people sleep, their dreaming is an effort to resolve psychological problems, to discharge tension, and to maintain sleep. The workings of unconscious anxiety may be seen in a number of different ways:

- Suppose a three-year-old child, drinking milk from a glass, bites and shatters the edge of the glass. The glass cuts the child's lip, which bleeds profusely. Striving to remain calm, the mother places a compress under the lip and stops the bleeding. But she does not know whether the child has swallowed any of the glass and, therefore, what she should do next. She asks the child if he has swallowed glass. He says he has not. To be certain, she asks again, saying, "Please tell me if you have, because if you have, you might have a tummyache, and we don't want you to have a tummyache." At this point the child says he *has* swallowed some glass. Now the mother does not know whether he has.

  Before the mother can decide that she had better take the child to the hospital, he begins to quiver as if shaking from the cold. This shaking is involuntary. Though the child has no conscious understanding of the possible fatal danger of swallowing glass and though the mother has tried to remain calm, unconsciously the child has sensed the inherent threat in the situation. Automatically, emergency physiological and biochemical processes are called into play to cope with the danger. We see the effects of these in the shaking. The manner and attitude of the hospital physician assure the child that there is no threat and gradually the shaking subsides.

- Adults may have the same experience in many different ways. Suppose as you drive your car down the street, a youngster dashes out from between parked cars into your path. You immediately slam on the brakes. For a moment you do not know whether you have hit the child. When you get out of the car, you see that you have not; but you find yourself shaking, your heart beating rapidly, your skin perspiring. You did not consciously cause any of these things to happen. The threat to your equilibrium—constituting stress-aroused anxiety, which in turn mobilized your resources for dealing with the emergency. A similar experience is commonplace among athletes. Some of them experience such psychological tension before competitive events that they cannot eat; if they do, they throw up.

Here I am speaking of conscious anxiety at one level. We are aware of certain threats and react to them. But at another, unconscious level, our reaction is disproportionate to the event. There is no objective reason for the driver to continue to be anxious after discovering that he or she has not hit the child. The overt threat is past. Yet the person may continue to shake for hours and may even dream or have nightmares about the event. It is understandable that athletes would want to win a game for conscious reasons. Why the competition should cause such a violent physical reaction is a more complex and obscure problem. They themselves do not know why they must go to such extremes of defensive mobilization that their bodies cannot tolerate the ingestion of food. Unconscious anxiety is at work.

EGO DEFENSES

If we are to penetrate deeply enough into Bob Lyons's reasons for suicide, we must go beyond admitting that he was undoubtedly anxious and under stress. We need to see why his ego was not sufficiently protected from such a completely destructive attack—why the defense mechanisms mentioned earlier as one of the ego's assistants did not enable him to overcome his anxiety.

A number of personality mechanisms operate automatically to help the ego maintain or regain its equilibrium. These mechanisms may be viewed as falling into three broad classes:

1. One group has to do with shaping or forming the personality. Included in this category is *identification*, the process of behaving like someone else. For example, a man identifies himself with his boss when he

dresses or speaks as his boss does. Women identify themselves with a leading movie star when they adopt her hairstyle. Another device, *introjection,* is a stronger form of identification, although the line between them is hazy. One who introjects the mannerisms or attitudes of another makes these firmly a part of himself or herself. We speak of introjecting the values of the parents and becoming a "chip off the old block."

2. Another group of mechanisms is universally used. These devices are required to control, guide, refine, and channel the basic drives or impulses from the id. I have already talked about *repression.* Another mechanism, *sublimation,* is the process by which basic drives are refined and directed into acceptable channels. Lyons, for example, sublimated much of his aggressive drive into his work.

3. A third group of mechanisms is made up of temporary devices that are called into play automatically when there is some threat to the personality.

Denial, a form of repression, is one of these devices and can be clarified by an example.

Suppose a plant superintendent has five years to go to retirement, and his boss suggests that he pick a successor and train him. But our plant superintendent does not select a successor, despite repeated requests from the boss. He cannot "hear" what the boss is saying and may be forced to select such a man. When the time for retirement arrives, he may then say to his boss that the boss really did not intend to retire him. He cannot believe the boss will compel him to leave. This behavior reflects a denial of the reality of the situation because the ego has difficulty accepting what it regards to be a loss of love (status, esteem, etc.).

Rationalization is another temporary mechanism that all of us use from time to time. In fact, as the following example shows, it provides the subject matter for comedy.

A man's wife suggests that it is time to get a new car because theirs is already eight years old and getting shabby. At first, acting under the influence of the superego, the man doubts if he needs a new car. He cannot justify it to himself. To buy one without an adequate reason would be a waste of money for him. "You're too mature to be so extravagant and to fall for style," his superego says. The guilt aroused by the thought of buying a new car (a form of anxiety) causes the idea to be rejected to appease the superego. The old car still runs well, he says; it gives no trouble, and a new one would be expensive. Soon we see him in an automobile showroom. "Just looking," he tells the salesman. "He thinks he's found a sucker," he chuckles to himself to avoid the condemnation of the superego. Next, however, he begins to complain to his wife and friends that the old car will soon need repairs, that it will never be worth more on a trade-in. Before long he has developed a complete rationale for buying the new car and has convinced himself to do so.

Projection, another temporary mechanism, is the process of attributing one's own feelings to someone else. If, for example, one can project hostility onto someone else ("He's mad at me; he's out to get me"), then one can justify to the superego that hostility toward the other person ("It's all right for me to get him first"). This is one mechanism behind scapegoating and prejudice.

Idealization is the process of putting a halo around someone else and thereby being unable to see his or her faults. This process is seen most vividly in people who are in love or who have identified strongly with political leaders. It enhances the image of the idealized person as a source of strength and gratification.

Reaction formation is a formidable term for the process of doing the opposite of what one wants to do to avoid the threat of giving free rein to impulses. Some people become so frightened of their own aggressive impulses that they act in an extremely meek manner, avoiding any suggestion of aggression.

Another important mechanism is *substitution,* or displacement. This is the process in which the ego, unable to direct impulses to the appropriate target, directs them to a substitute target. In a benign way, this happens when people devote much of their affection to pets or to their work if, for whatever reasons, they do not have satisfactory ways of giving affection to other people. More destructive displacement occurs when a person seeks substitute targets for aggression. For instance, if unable to express anger at his boss to the boss, a man may displace it onto the working conditions or wages. He may even unwittingly carry it home and criticize his wife or children. This is another mechanism behind scapegoating and prejudice. Not only does displacement of this kind hurt others; worse yet, it doesn't contribute to the solution of the real problem.

Compensation is still another mechanism—often highly constructive. This is the process of developing talents and skills to make up for one's unconsciously perceived or imagined deficiencies or of undertaking activities and relationships to regain lost gratification. In certain respects, compensation and substitution are, of course, closely related.

The Defensive Process

These mechanisms need not be elaborated further here. The answer to why Bob Lyons killed himself has necessarily been delayed long enough. Now we see the point, however. When the ego is threatened in some fashion, anxiety spontaneously and unconsciously triggers mechanisms to counteract the threat. If there are too many emergencies for the personality, it may then overuse these mechanisms, and this in turn will seriously distort the person's view of reality or cripple him or her psychologically. To identify with those one respects is fine; to imitate them slavishly is to lose one's individuality. It is one thing to rationalize occasionally, as we all do, but another to base judgments consistently on rationalizations. At times all of us project our own feelings, but we would be sick indeed if we felt most of the time that everyone else had it in for us.

By and large, self-fulfillment has to do with the ego's capacity to function as effectively as it can. When emotional conflicts can be diminished and the need for defensiveness can be decreased, the energy that ordinarily maintains the defenses is freed for more useful activity. In a sense, some of the brakes are removed from the psychological wheels. Furthermore, as threats are removed and the defenses need no longer be used so intensely, one perceives reality more accurately. One can then relate to other people more reasonably and communicate more clearly. A psychological blossoming can occur. When such balancing fails to take place, the ego is overwhelmed for the time being. In Bob Lyons's case, he acted to relieve his emotional pain and killed himself before equilibrium could be restored in a less destructive way. Since this balancing process is the ultimate key to an understanding of Lyons's act, let us make sure we understand how it works and then apply our knowledge directly to his case:

Fusion of drives toward appropriate target—Suppose a man is called into his boss's office, and his boss criticizes him harshly for something he did not do. The ideally healthy man, if he exists, will listen calmly to what his boss has to say and, in good control of his rising aggressive impulse, might well reply, "I'm sorry that such a mistake has happened. I had nothing to do with that particular activity, but perhaps I can help you figure out a way to keep the same mistake from happening again." His boss, also brimming with good mental health, might then respond, "I'm sorry that I criticized you unfairly. I would appreciate your giving me a hand on this." Together they direct their energies toward the solution of the problem.

Displacement to less appropriate target—But take a similar situation where, however, the man knows his boss will brook no contradiction or is so emotionally overwrought that there is little point in trying to be reasonable with him. This man may fume with anger at the unjust attack but control his impulse to strike back at the boss. His reality-testing ego tells him that such action won't help the situation at all. He takes the criticism, anticipating a better solution when the boss cools off. Nevertheless, he is angry for being unjustly criticized, and there has been no opportunity to discharge his aroused aggressive impulse in an appropriate way toward the solution of the problem.

Because in this situation it seems so rational to control one's impulse (i.e., the boss is upset and there's no point in discussing it with him now), the ego finds this secondary anger an inappropriate feeling to allow into consciousness. The more primitive secondary anger is then repressed. When the employee goes bowling that night, he gets particular pleasure from knocking the pins down, without knowing why. Unconsciously he is using bowling to drain off his excess aggression. Such displacement is a partially constructive way of discharging aggression: it hurts no one and provides gratification. However, it does not contribute directly to resolving the problem itself, presuming that some further action toward solution might be required.

Containment of drives—Suppose that another man finds himself in the same situation. This man has learned in the course of growing up that it is not permissible to express one's aggression directly to authority figures. Being human, he has aggressive impulses, but, having a severe superego, he also feels guilty about them and goes to great lengths to repress them. When the boss criticizes him and his aggressive impulse is stimulated, repression automatically sets in, and the impulse is controlled without his being aware of it. However, it is so controlled that he can't speak up to contribute to the solution of the problem.

Because this man constantly maintains a high degree of control to meet the demands of his superego, he is already in a potentially more explosive situation, ready to defend himself from the slightest possible threat. If he has to contain more of his anger within himself, the situation is much like rising steam pressure in a boiler. If this situation is repetitive or chronic, the mobilization and remobilization of defenses almost require of the ego that it be in a steady emergency state. The alarm bells are ringing most of the time. This kind of reaction strains the ego's resources and is particularly wearing physiologically because each psychological response to stress is accompanied by physiological mobilization, too.

Psychosomatic symptoms result. The body is literally damaged by its own nervous system and fluids, leading to ulcers, hypertension, and similar phenomena. This experience is commonly recognized in the phrase "stewing in one's own juice." Clinical data seem to show that there are reasons why one particular organ is the site for a psychosomatic symptom, but often these reasons are obscure.

Displacement onto the self—Take another man, who also has learned that aggression should not be expressed to others and who cannot do so without feelings of guilt. In fact, his superego won't tolerate much hostility on his part, so he lives constantly with feelings of guilt. The guilt, in turn, makes him feel inadequate as his superego repeatedly berates him for his hostility. No matter how nice he may try to be, by means of reaction formation, he can't satisfy his superego. Somehow, he himself always seems to be at fault. With such a rigid, punitive superego, this man under the same kind of attack may then respond by saying, "I guess you're right. I'm always wrong; it's my fault. I never seem to do things right." He may also then have a mild depression. Depression is always an indication of anger with one's self, originating from anger toward another, and reflects the attack of the superego on the ego. The aggression is displaced from the appropriate target back onto the self and results in a form of self-blame and self-punishment.

Another form of self-attack or self-punishment is seen in many accidents. Most of them are not actually accidents in the sense that they occur by chance but are unconscious modes of self-punishment. "Forgetting" to turn the motor switch off before repairing the machine or not seeing or hearing possible threats frequently indicates that denial or repression has been operating in order to permit the person to hurt himself or herself to appease the superego. In extreme form, this self-directed aggression is the mechanism behind suicide, and now we are prepared to see what happened to Bob Lyons.

The Reason Why

Driven by an extremely severe superego, Bob Lyons sublimated his drives successfully in his work as long as he could work hard. There was an equilibrium among ego, superego, id, and environment, although only a tenuous one. By driving himself, he could appease the superego's relentless pressure.

Such a superego, however, is never satisfied. Its demands arise from unconscious sources, which, because they are unconscious, probably have existed from early childhood and are to a large extent irrational. If they were not irrational, their terms could be met.

Whenever he reached a goal toward which he had aspired, Lyons got no satisfaction from it, for his superego still drove him. And when he could no longer work as hard as he had, this for him was an environmental deprivation. He could no longer earn love by performing well. His superego became more relentless. The vacation, which placed no demands on him at all, simply added to his guilt and feelings of unworthiness and inadequacy. With sublimations and displacements reduced, given his kind of superego, his aggressive drive had only the ego as a major target.

And, at that moment, the only way that Bob Lyons knew to appease his superego was to kill himself.

Had his superego developed differently, Lyons might have achieved as he did because of ego reasons (the pleasure and gratification he got from his work), with a mild assist from the superego to do well. When his superego developed so strongly, probably because of a heavy burden of hostility in childhood for which he felt irrationally guilty for a lifetime, there was no real pleasure in what he did and nothing more than temporary gratification. The relentless driving of himself was a form of self-sacrifice—just like alcoholism, most accidents, repeated failures on the job, presenting the worst side of one's self to others, and some forms of crime.

We should recognize that a bit of self-sacrifice exists in all of us, just as we can see something of ourselves at times in each of the preceding three examples. The ancient observation that "man is his own worst enemy" is testimony to the self-destructive potential in each person. Bob Lyons differed from the rest of us only in degree and only because of a combination of forces at a given point that precipitated his death. A change in any single force might conceivably have prevented it: more and harder work, psychiatric or psychological treatment, no vacation to add to the feelings of guilt and uselessness, or open recognition by his physician of the seriousness of mental illness.

GROPING FOR SHADOWS

But how would his physician or friends have recognized early symptoms of Lyons's illness? It would not have been easy. We cannot put an ego under a microscope or locate the id in any part of the body. These are simply names given to what seem to be systems of forces operating in the personality. We cannot see repression—it is only a name for the observation that some things are forgotten and can be recalled only under certain circumstances. The same is true when we speak of something being unconscious. It is not relegated to a given physical organ or place. One is merely not able to call it into awareness.

If the ego has a constant balancing task and calls certain mechanisms into play to carry it out, the ego, being concerned with psychological economy, will develop mechanisms that are preferred because they work best consistently. These become the established personality traits. As individuals we make our preferred modes of adjustment those ways of behaving that are most comfortable (least anxiety arousing) to us.

The consistent modes of adjustment, the personality traits, become the hallmarks by which we are known to others. Even physical styles of behavior become part of this system. If we hear on the telephone a voice that we recognize, we can place it with a name. If we meet a friend we have not seen in 10 years, we will observe that he or she seems to be same as always—talking, reacting, thinking in much the same way. Some are hail-fellow-well-met gregarious types, others more diffident and conservative. Each has preferred modes of adjustment, preferred ways to consistently maintain equilibrium.

Given these entrenched modes of adaptation, even clinical psychologists and psychiatrists are unlikely to make *radical* changes in people, although they can often help alter certain forces so that people can behave more healthily than they did previously. The alteration of internal forces (superego-ego-id) is the job of the clinician. But individuals often can make a contribution to the alteration of external forces (ego-environment). Even minor changes in the balance of forces can significantly affect how people feel, think, and behave.

The very fact that people do not radically change their styles of behavior makes it possible to detect signs of emotional stress. Given certain characteristic modes of adaptation in the form of personality traits, a person who experiences some kind of emotional stress is likely first to make greater use of those mechanisms that worked best before. The first sign of defense against stress is that a person seems to be conspicuously more like always. A person who is ordinarily quiet may become withdrawn under stress. If like Lyons, his or her first reaction may well be to try to work harder.

Second, if this line of defense does not work well (or if the stress is too severe or chronic for that method alone), inefficient psychological functioning begins to appear—vague fears, inability to concentrate, compulsions to do certain things, increasing irritability, and declining work performance. We will also see the results of physiological defensive efforts. We saw in Lyons's case that tension, jitteriness, and inability to hold food or to sleep all accompanied his psychological stress. The whole organism—physiological and psychological—was involved in the struggle.

Psychological and physiological symptoms are ways of "binding" or attempting to control the anxiety. They are ways of trying to do something about a problem, however ineffective they may be. And they are the best ways of dealing with the problem that a person has available at the moment, though better ways of coping may be apparent to others who do not have the same psychological makeup. That's why it is dangerous to try to remove symptoms. Instead, it is wiser to resolve the underlying problem.

Third, if neither of these types of defenses can contain the anxiety, we may see sharp changes in personality. A person no longer behaves as before. Lyons felt himself to be falling apart, unable to work as he did previously. A neat person may become slovenly, an efficient one alcoholic. Radical changes in personality indicate severe illness, which usually requires hospitalization.

Conspicuous change in behavior indicates that the ego is no longer able to maintain effective control. If a person is so upset that he or she hears voices or sees things that do not exist, previously unconscious thoughts and feelings are breaking through. Obviously irrational behavior indicates the same thing. There is a loss of contact with reality, seriously impaired judgment, and an inability to be responsible for oneself. In such a state, Bob Lyons committed suicide.

Conclusion

Now that we *think* we understand why Bob Lyons killed himself, it is important that two cautions be raised.

ABOUT OURSELVES

First, readers newly exposed to psychoanalytic theory invariably fall victim to what may be called the freshman medical student's syndrome: they get every symptom in the book. Everything to which this article refers, average readers will be able to see in themselves. As we were discussing Lyons, we were talking about human beings and human motivation; so it was inevitable that we ended up talking about ourselves. We must recognize this tendency to read ourselves into these pages and compensate for it by consciously trying to maintain an objective distance from the material.

At the same time, does this very experience not make it clear to us that everyone has the continuing task of maintaining an equilibrium? At any given time, any one of us may be listing to starboard a little or trying to keep from being buffeted about by a sudden storm. Despite these pressures, we must nevertheless move forward, correcting for the list as best we can or conserving our strength to ride out the storm. Each will defend himself or herself the best way he or she knows how—the more energy devoted to defense, the less available for forward movement.

Each of us at one time or another, therefore, will be emotionally disturbed or upset. For a few hours, a few days, a few weeks, we may be irritable or angry ("I got up on the wrong side of the bed"), blue ("I'm feeling low today"), or hypersensitive. When we feel these ways, when we are having difficulty maintaining an equilibrium, for that brief period we are emotionally disturbed. We cannot work as well as we usually do. It is more difficult for us to sustain our relationships with other people. We may feel hopeless or helpless. We're just not ourselves.

But just because we are mildly emotionally disturbed does not mean we need professional help or hospitalization. A cold is a minor form of upper respiratory infection, the extreme of which is pneumonia. If one has a cold, that does not mean he or she will have pneumonia. Even if a person does get pneumonia, with present treatment methods most people recover; and the same is true of mental illness. The difference between the mild and the severe is one of degree, not of kind.

Because each of us is human and no one of us has had either perfect heredity or perfect environment, each of us has weak spots. When the balance of forces is such that there is stress where we are weak, we will have difficulty. The incidence of mental illness, then, is not 1 out of 20 or some other proportionate statistic. Rather it is 1 out of 1!

WHAT WE CAN DO

The second caution has to do with the limitations of this exposition and the reader's preparation for understanding it. This necessarily has been a highly condensed version of some aspects of psychoanalytic theory. Many important aspects of the theory have been omitted, and others have been presented without the many qualifications a serious scientific presentation would require. The reader should therefore look on what is presented only as an introduction to better understanding of psychological problems, should be careful about overgeneralization, and should studiously avoid using jargon or interpreting people's behavior to them.

Without observing these limitations, the inexperienced person will be unable to help anyone. Within these limitations, however, executives can render extremely important help to others in their companies—and to themselves. Specifically, they can recognize that:

- *All* behavior is motivated, much of it by thoughts and feelings of which the person is not aware. Behavior does not occur by chance.

- At any one time each person is doing the best he or she can, as a result of the multiple forces that bring about any given behavior. A change in the forces is required to bring about a change in behavior.

- Love neutralizes aggression and diminishes hostility. "A soft word turneth away wrath," says the old aphorism. Love does not mean maudlin expressions but actions that reflect esteem and regard for the other person as a human being. The most useful demonstration of affection is support that takes the form of:

    Understanding that the pain of emotional distress is real. It will not go away by wishing it away, by dismissing it as "all in your head,' or by urging the person to "forget it," "snap out of it," or "take a vacation."

    Listening if people bring problems to you or if problems so impair their work that you must criticize their work performance. Listening permits people to define their problems more clearly and thereby to examine courses of action. Acting constructively to solve a problem is the best way the ego has to maintain the fusion of drives in dealing with reality. Listening, by providing some relief for distressed people, already brings about some alteration in the balance of forces.

    If you listen, however, you must clearly recognize your limitations: (1) you can offer only emergency help; (2) you cannot hold yourself *responsible* for other people's personal problems, some of which would defy the most competent specialist.

    Referring the troubled person to professional sources of help if the problem is more than temporary or if the person is severely upset. Every organization should have channels for referral. A person who has responsibility for other people but no formal organizational channels for referral would do well to establish contact with a psychiatrist, a clinical psychologist, or a community mental health agency. Professional sources of guidance will then be available when problems arise.

Finally, we can maintain a watchful, but not morbid, eye on ourselves. If we find that we are having difficulties that interfere with our work or with gratifying relationships with other people, then we should be wise enough to seek professional help.

Handling the Constructive Drive

In this article, because we are focusing on Bob Lyons's case, we are looking at ways in which the ego deals with the *aggressive* drive by calling into play certain defense mechanisms in order to maintain its equilibrium. But the ego also must deal with the *constructive* drive in order to maintain the proper balance. We see how it might handle sexual stimulation by control and refinement, or even denial, of the impulse. Other examples illustrate how the same mechanisms that are used to cope with the aggressive drive apply themselves to handling constructive drives and, in so doing, often cause us distress as well as relief:

1. *Fusion of drives.* Fused with the aggressive drive, and dominant over it, the constructive drive is directed toward appropriate targets in intimate relationships with one's family, the solution of work and family problems, citizenship activities, and so on. Idealistic love without an aggressive component might lead to merely fantasized images of a sweetheart rather than marriage, or a person might dream about job success rather than take action toward it.

2. *Displacement to less appropriate targets.* Like the aggressive drive, the constructive drive may be deflected from appropriate targets. Homosexuality is one such phenomenon whose dynamics are too complex for discussion here. In brief, many psychoanalytic clinicians theorize that the homosexual cannot establish adequate and satisfying relationships with those of the opposite sex. Instead, he or she uses the mechanism of substitution and builds up extended rationalizations to appease the superego.

    Some people can invest themselves in causes but not really in other people. Some lavish great affection on animals or houses or hobbies at the expense of personal relationships. Some adults can have affectionate relationships only with young children but cannot tolerate other adults. These targets provide useful channels for love but not the fully satisfying, wide range of relationships enjoyed by most mature adults.

3. *Containment.* Some people, for complicated reasons, learned that it was psychologically safe not to express affection and have repressed their affectionate feelings. These people we know colloquially as "cold fish," people seemingly without emotion. They may be highly intellectual or great professional successes, but they have divorced compassion from judgment and feeling from reasoning. Others are known as ruthlessly efficient. They keep their emotions tightly controlled and their feelings of love deeply buried within themselves.

4. *Displacement onto the self.* Children rejected by their parents learn bitterly that it is too painful to try to love other people because they will not return love. In adult life, such people become highly self-centered. In conversation they constantly talk about themselves. They give overmeticulous attention to their appearance and revel in self-display. They tend to seek out activities which provide public adulation and become extremely unhappy when they cannot get it. We find such people unpleasant to deal with because they are unable to give anything of themselves to someone else. Often they exploit others for their own gain. Because they cannot love others, they have almost no real friends and often are unable to sustain their marriages.

For these people much of the constructive drive is displaced onto themselves because environmental forces have made identification and introjection difficult, thereby impairing the possibility of relationships with other people. The early conflicts, now repressed, still exist unconsciously. Their egos—remembering early pain—will not open again to the possibilities of rejection and narrowly constrict the constructive drive to a limited target for self-protection. Because of the limited range of attachments their egos permit, such people do not really enjoy life, despite what appears to others to be an extremely sparkling series of social adventures.

Each person must have a certain amount of self-love if he or she is to have self-respect. Overweening egocentricity, however, is ultimately destructive because of the absence of gratification, because of the pain caused other people, and because it diverts energy from social contributions the person could make.

An extreme form of egocentricity is hypochondriasis. Some people invest all of their energy in themselves in an extremely distorted way by being preoccupied with their own bodies. They are never free of aches and pains, often spending years and untold dollars "doctoring." They sacrifice most of life's pleasures to nurse their fancied ills, undeterred by repeated medical reports that show there is no need for surgery or that they do not have cancer, and the like. In some respects, such people commit slow suicide as they cut themselves off more and more from the outside world. In some cases, they will even allow one or more limbs to atrophy from disuse because they claim it is too painful to walk or to move.

Retrospective Commentary

Since Freud published his first psychoanalytic work 81 years ago, quarrel and debate have raged over the theory's validity and usefulness. It has long been rejected as fantasy by most academic psychologists, declared conceptually inconsistent by certain philosophers, and denounced as unscientific by some researchers.

Nevertheless, despite its limitations and inadequacies, psychoanalytic theory continues to be the most comprehensive explanation that is presently available of how and why people behave as they do. It helps us understand and predict complex behavior better than any other existing theory and has led to a good deal of significant research in the field (which many people choose to ignore). From its earliest days, it has spawned a host of subtheories and partial theories—including such contemporary offshoots as transactional analysis, Gestalt psychology, and others. I am of course pleased—but not surprised— that the theory outlined in "What Killed Bob Lyons?" endures, more because of the usefulness of the theory itself than my adaptation and application of it.

Why has psychoanalytic theory endured? Most theoretical efforts to explain people's feelings, thinking, and behavior are of two kinds. First, what Kurt Eissler calls *medial* theories assume external motivation—that people are pushed, pulled, shaped, stretched, condensed (whatever the metaphors may be) by external forces. Tacitly, they accept John Locke's dictum that man is a tabula rasa—or smooth, blank tablet—to be written on by the fates.

Medial theories include reward/punishment or stimulus/response psychological theories and sociological role theories. All these have some validity but simply do not go far enough because they do not account for what goes on *within* individuals—what feelings and thoughts (particularly unconscious processes) impel and propel a person to interact with external forces. They work only to the degree one can control the environment. Since there aren't many environments these days that can be well controlled, such theories are severely limited and inadequate when one seeks to apply them to complex interpersonal subtleties. One may apply reward contingencies to a few people, but no senior manager has time to figure out such contingencies for his or her subordinates even if they were to work. And no role is so rigidly defined that everyone who performs it is compelled to do it in the same way.

Second are *normative* theories, which apply to everybody. However, what applies to everybody in general applies to nobody specifically. To use a normative theory is like saying that the mean temperature of Boston is 68°. But it may not be 68° on any given day, nor will the mean help you understand whether it is likely to rain or whether you should wear overshoes.

Abraham Maslow's hierarchy of needs is an example of a normative theory that enables us to understand generalized behaviors. However, it does not allow for interventions of choice, e.g., what is the best thing to do about a specific person with a specific problem under a specific set of circumstances.

Self-actualization, the highest of Maslow's needs, is frequently equated with autonomy. Managers are urged to give their subordinates greater autonomy so that they can actualize themselves. Obviously, though, many people in this world have not actualized themselves simply by being autonomous. Besides, nobody really knows who has achieved self-actualization because nobody knows exactly what it is.

While it is important for managers to know about psychological theories, they quickly become frustrated with the limitations of those theories. They need to make definitive decisions about individuals and groups and must resolve specific problems under specific circumstances. Highway road maps are simply not sufficient when one must grasp the topography of the terrain.

Only something as comprehensive as psychoanalytic theory can explain why Bob Lyons committed suicide or can be extrapolated to gain a better grasp of a whole gamut of managerial issues. The theory helps us understand and act on such diverse concerns as understanding stress, dealing with emotional conflicts, selecting leaders, appraising performance, and compensating employees. No other theory of personality covers the wide range of human behavior in organizations.

People are not merely blank tablets. They give meaning to the internal and external stimuli that impinge on them, and they react to those stimuli in terms of that meaning. They are not merely occupants of roles who behave as the roles presumably require them to. They act on and modify those roles in keeping with what goes on in their own heads. The specificity and depth of these internal processes, which then lead to complex interactions with external forces, are missing from contemporary behavioral science theories. As a result, the theories fall short in providing managers with specifics for action that have consistency across problems. Furthermore, inconsistent assumptions lead, predictably, to conflicts. For example, people cannot cooperate effectively if they are being paid to compete with each other.

One reason that psychoanalytic theory has not died is because it is continuously evolving. Six major trends have become prominent in recent years:

1. An important development is the recognition of the complexity of a person's attachment to a "significant other." A great deal of work has been done since World War II—in England based on the theories of Melanie Klein, and in this country based on the work of Margaret Mahler—in studying how infants attach themselves to the caring figures around them. Children not only form such attachments but also incorporate images of the figures into their own memories. They try to integrate those images into consistent patterns of behavior that serve as models for the cores of their developing personalities. If these attachments are disrupted—for example, by transient caretakers or rejecting mothers or if children are separated from parents by war or other factors—then it is difficult for children to integrate the range of these images into a coherent pattern. Their personalities will therefore be inconsistent.

    Because they have experienced such disruptions and because of a number of other societal forces, many people have become intensely preoccupied with themselves and their own needs and have difficulty attaching themselves to others and maintaining consistent relationships. Tom Wolfe has called this phenomenon the "me generation," and Christopher Lasch writes of "the culture of narcissism." The two most prominent psychoanalytic theorists in this area are Heinz Kohut and Otto Kernberg.

2. Psychoanalytic theory originally was a drive theory, that is, it gave great attention to forces pushing from within and to making conscious that which was unconscious. More recently, the concept of ego psychology—concern with how people adapt—has become increasingly important. The two dominant theorists in this area are the late Heinz Hartman and David Rapaport. Much contemporary psychoanalytic practice centers on helping people understand why they don't adapt as well as they would like and on helping them evolve better ways of coping with themselves and their environments. Since "What Killed Bob Lyons?" was written, a new preoccupation with stress, stress relief, and stress prevention has arisen. Ego psychology gives particular meaning and understanding to the problem of stress, which is often naively viewed merely as a product of external forces.

3. Erik Erikson's concept of developmental stages was followed by the work of Daniel Levinson, George Vaillant, and others who refined understanding of personality development. Their research calls our attention both to the continuity of such development throughout life and to the importance of transitions from one phase to another, particularly during and after middle age.

    Contemporary concern with career development, mid-career changes, and the concepts of "burnout" and occupational satiation has made self-understanding imperative if a person is going to be free to make choices about his or her own direction and life. The contemporary ethos, with its heavy emphasis on personal choice, simply highlights the need for self-understanding.

4. Concern with developing and preserving executive talent has increased. So has recognition of the psychological bases underlying heart disease, suicides, accidents, alcoholism, and a wide range of maladaptive behaviors. The frequency and seriousness of these costly problems contribute to the urgency to understand them better. The increasing intensity of change in our society and the disruption caused by inevitable change have also given impetus to people's wish to cope more effectively. Such concepts as the Holmes and Rahe scale of life-change events, the Friedman and Rosenman delineation of Type A behavior, and the results of research into plant closings, occupational hazards, organizational status, and role conflict have all helped understanding of such issues.

5. Major work on family therapy (by Nathan Ackerman, John Bell, and Murray Bowen, among others) and on group therapy (by Wilfred Bion and others) has provided a psychoanalytic basis for conflict resolution that may be extended to organizations. This work is important because many conflicts cannot be resolved without understanding the unconscious forces that underlie them. Conflicts in our society have also escalated, and many people would like to resolve them more effectively.

6. Increasing theoretical attention has been given to the role of the father in the family. This has implications for role modeling for both boys and girls and for the rivalry that evolves between sons and fathers, the so-called Oedipus complex. Its implications for leadership have been discussed by Abraham Zaleznik and in some of my own work.

If I were to rewrite my article today, I would want to include these recent developments. I would continue to bring psychoanalytic theory into contemporary perspective by applying it to a wide range of current topics and problems. In my writing, I have tried to explain why performance appraisals uniformly fail; why attitude surveys, morale studies, and other efforts to understand work satisfaction are severely limited; why efforts to improve the quality of work life frequently founder. I've tried also to build on the concept of the ego ideal—the image of ourselves toward which we all strive. The gap between the ego ideal and the self-image is a measure of self-esteem. The greater the gap, the greater the anger with self—and therefore the greater the stress.

Psychoanalytic theory does not provide all the answers to all these problems, but it is a way to look at them and to open some avenues for thinking about them. Whether psychoanalytic theory is right or wrong is not even a question. Theories are not right or wrong. They either enable one to understand and predict or they don't. Fundamentally, the only question is whether a theory is useful; if it is, one then has a frame of reference about motivation that he or she can apply in the same way as a frame of reference about marketing, finance, economics, production, or control. I have found psychoanalytic theory useful and have therefore tried to make it increasingly so for others.

Reprint 81206

Originally published in 1963, republished in March–April 1981.

5
Criteria for Choosing Chief Executives

No one person has all qualities of an ideal leader. No one is at one time farseeing, sensitive, analytical, energetic, well-spoken, active, wise, and involved. Real people are more like diamonds, this author maintains, with facets of personality, and flaws. Also some dimensions of personality are more important than others depending on the company and its environment. What the author offers here is a list of 20 dimensions that he has found most important most often, and a scale of characteristics to use in evaluating behavior against the dimensions. The author offers this list with a few caveats, however; the list like people, like diamonds, is itself not perfect; it is not all-inclusive, and it is not sanctioned by any authority but his own experience.

"Did I find it frustrating as the White House Chief of Staff? Toughest job I ever had, but . . . if you find it unpleasant to cope with a complex problem that is simultaneously the business of four or five Cabinet departments, several public interest groups, and the Congress, and one that the President will finally decide, then it's frustrating. On the other hand, if you like that situation, if it's a challenge, then it's stimulating, particularly when you see progress made. I found it tough, challenging, exhausting, but not frustrating." (Donald Rumsfeld, president and chief executive, G.D. Searle and Company)[1]

"Executives like David Mahoney and Ray Kroc aren't clairvoyants, but often they 'see' ways to solve business problems that defy computer logic. The bottom-line results can be spectacular."[2]

"Ironically, ITT's directors felt that Mr. Hamilton's leadership in the telecommunications area, as well as others, lacked the conviction they wanted, various ITT sources said . . . And forceful leadership at ITT is as critical as ever, the directors believe, because of vigorous competition from abroad. . . ."[3]

"'Dick [Giordano] is very bright, able, and well-organized, and he knows how to bring out the best in people,' says Robert H. Legg, a former Airco director and retired chairman of Uris Brothers. Adds Airco director Crocker Nevin, executive director of Drexel Burnham Lambert, Inc.: 'Dick is a masterful student of people and their abilities.'"[4]

"Henry Singleton is supremely indifferent to criticism . . . During the '70s, when investors and brokers alike lost their enthusiasm and deserted Teledyne, Singleton had Teledyne buy up its own stock. . . . Between October 1972 and February 1976 he reduced Teledyne's outstanding common 64% from 32 million shares to 11.4 million. He didn't shift course according to Wall Street pressures, even against the advice of his own board, while other CEOs backed off."[5]

A person having the desirable characteristics reflected in these vignettes would be attractive to any CEO or board with the task of looking for a successor or selecting a chief executive. If you are pondering the choice of a successor or considering the development of a range of candidates for high-level advancement, how can you assure yourself that the person you select will have the characteristics that will make him or her the best person for a given time?

Of course, you will ask the usual questions: What are you selecting the person to do? For how long? What issues will have to take a secondary place? What trade-offs are you making? What are the crucial factors about the organization that influence your deliberation? What is currently the organization's dominant competitive edge? How has the organization "made it" in the past? What is likely to be its dominant competitive edge in the future? At what stage is this organization in its growth and development?[6] What then are its pressing developmental tasks?

What do you think the business environment will be five or ten years from now? What particular problems do these environments pose for this organization? What problems has the organization had in the past that likely to recur? How would you describe the character or style of the organization? What kinds of people fit here?

Your answers to these questions among others constitute a job description for a chief executive. Your next task then is to determine the kinds of competence and the range of behavior a person should have to do what you have already defined. Obviously, the idea that a good manager can manage anything is nonsense, as much contemporary divestiture demonstrates. Accordingly, the next step is to evaluate candidates. That requires looking more closely at the subtleties of behavior that differentiate those who have significant leadership potential from those who do not. To do that requires some way of examining the behavior of prospective candidates. That is no mean task, first, because there are no agreed-on criteria, and second, because even if there were, no one person could meet such standards.

Some criteria, however, might be helpful in this process. Even though psychologists, personnel people, and executives do not agree about what are the ideal characteristics of a candidate for top management, let alone on how to classify behavior, experience nevertheless offers some possibilities.

The exhibit displays a list of personality dimensions, together with a set of scales as an aid to judgment. I offer them with several caveats: I make no claim for statistical validation of the dimensions or that the scales represent equal intervals or accurate measures. Without agreement on classification, there can't be agreement on measures or ranking. (I am assuming that the candidates judged against these dimensions will have, at a minimum, business competence; a decision-making role, where the buck has stopped, before the age of 35; and a personal history that reflects early winning or achievement experiences.) The dimensions, therefore, should be used qualitatively, not as an arithmetic index. In fact, you may want to substitute some ideas of your own at various scale intervals. Such a list is not intended to be a set of criteria to which people are held, with the expectation of near perfection on all dimensions. Rather, it is a way of calling attention to and examining facets or dimensions of personality that relate to executive success.

Several other caveats come to mind:

- A good executive is multifaceted like a diamond. The larger the number of facets, the more brilliantly it shines. Some facets are larger, some smaller. And not all diamonds have the same number. But all facets are part of a whole diamond, which ultimately focuses the light passing through the facets to a single integrating point. Further, few diamonds are without flaws.
- Some aspects of behavior will be more significant for certain functions than for others. Sometimes these behavioral aspects will form a cluster. An aggressive, very controlling person who would fit one situation in an organization might be inappropriate in another. It is therefore more

useful to think of these dimensions not as individual measures or sums, but as configuration patterns or profiles. The appropriate question is, "What profile of dimensions best fits the profile of behavior required for the job description that I have drawn up?"

- People are always more complicated than the rubrics we use to describe them. Behavior is too elusive for fixed categories. All description therefore is approximation. A classification is a guide; pointing to certain features, it does not cover the whole territory. It is also static, and cannot describe a stream of actions in context. Furthermore, some of these dimensions overlap. The overlapping enables us to view subtleties just as turning the diamond lets us see another facet, though both lead to the same center.

I have organized 20 personality dimensions into three groups, according to psychological themes. (I leave out deeper and more subtle emotional aspects of the candidate's life experience because these are not the province of the layman.) In the first group, the dimensions have to do primarily with thinking. In the second, they are more related to feelings and interrelationships, particularly to the management of aggressive feelings; affection and the universal need to love and be loved; and dependency. Those in the third are more related to outward behavior characteristics. The order of the dimensions does not reflect their relative importance; that will hinge significantly on the organization's needs.

Dimensions of leaders' personalities

THINKING

1. Capacity to abstract, to conceptualize, to organize, and to integrate different data into a coherent frame of reference.	Thinks concretely, item by item, fact by fact.	Can organize facts into patterns and sequences, but doesn't relate sequences to arrive at concepts.	Can relate theory to management problems, but doesn't search out concepts and ideas.	Can criticize theory and use it for long-range thinking about business.	Encyclopedic synthesist, able to organize and integrate creatively principles, values, concepts, and information from full range of arts and sciences.
2. Tolerance for ambiguity, can stand confusion until things become clear.	Needs to keep focus on one defined project at a time.	Can handle several projects but with stress.	Can handle vague project guidelines, but must always be anchored to concrete structure or method.	Can work with unspecified goals and uncertainty as long as can return to concrete orienting point occasionally.	Can tolerate ambiguity for years, doesn't get anxious waiting for long-term plans to come to fruition.
3. Intelligence, has the capacity not only to abstract, but also to be practical.	Educated, but not very imaginative or creative.	Educated, but doesn't learn much from experience.	Bright, makes good use of experience. Sometimes might seem like a hustler.	Very intelligent, draws well on reservoir or experience.	Exceptionally bright, draws on a fountain of experience. Good street smarts.
4. Judgment, knows when to act.	Rushes to judgment, without thinking things through.	Sporadic, has made some terrible bloopers along the way.	Thoughtful, but never quite sees the whole picture or implications.	Good judgment, usually sees whole picture, but has blind spots in some areas.	Excellent judgment, very few mistakes over the years.

(continued)

Dimensions of leaders' personalities (*continued*)

FEELINGS AND INTERRELATIONSHIPS

5. Authority, has the feeling that he or she belongs in boss's role.	Bends over backward to please; can't give direction or control.	Can take charge when chips are down and become boss, but doesn't like to.	Doesn't apologize for being boss, but feels arrived at position by luck and is thus tentative.	Feels deserves to be boss, earned it, but also feels many others could do as well.	A "natural" in position. Takes full charge. Reasonably certain will do it well and probably better than most.
6. Activity, takes a vigorous orientation to problems and needs of the organization.	Reactive, moves when prodded. Often does not want to know information.	On occasion takes steps, but most often after having procrastinated and frustrated subordinates.	Attacks problems in fairly secure arenas, but takes little risk. Subordinates feel "not going any place."	Attacks problems tactically from new positions and consolidates forces. Subordinates willing to follow.	Attacks problems strategically, with well-defined targets. Plans long-term, step-by-step, inexorable advance ahead of competition.
7. Achievement, oriented toward organization's success rather than personal aggrandizement.	Wants to achieve, but passions don't match competence.	Great desire, but not willing to put out full effort for maximum achievement.	Intense wish to achieve that overflows into full effort, but competes too harshly and abrasively. May be ruthless. Strong need to control others.	Very motivated to achieve. Needs much external recognition, perquisites; feels defeated if not chosen. Doesn't need to overcontrol. Achievements are seen as personal, not organization's.	Very motivated to move upward as recognition of competence. May be disappointed if not chosen but not hungry for applause. Organization's achievements are seen as personal achievements.
8. Sensitivity, able to perceive subtleties of others' feelings.	Obtuse, can't read people's faces or their feelings between the lines of what they say.	Slow on the uptake. Dimly perceives feelings, but most often after the fact.	Picks up feelings and reads body movements, but sometimes too glibly, which may result in seeing feelings as superficial and manipulatable.	Anticipates responses and picks up group feelings. Aware more than most of the subtle cues, but second-guesses own responses to them.	Master at sensing feelings, anticipating them, and taking them seriously.

9. Involvement, sees oneself as a participating member of an organization.	Never leaves desk, won't go into the field.	Occasionally will appear in the field for ceremonial occasions.	Gets out sporadically, reluctantly, and perfunctorily, and doesn't learn much.	Goes into field regularly but not easily. Sees and touches but is felt to be distant by employees. Has difficulty drawing people out.	Allocates serious, continuing time to field visits. Mixes with employees, seeking information on their problems. Summarizes findings for employees and managers. Has finger on the pulse of the organization.
10. Maturity, has good relationships with authority figures.	Still an adolescent, always challenging bosses and resisting authority.	Armed truce with bosses, speaks up in hostile fashion under guise of honesty or tries to manipulate bosses.	Hard to predict. Sometimes has easy relationships, sometimes uncomfortable, depending on kind of boss.	Usually does well with bosses unless defensiveness is exacerbated by criticism or rivalry.	Works well with authority figures. Uniformly praised by all bosses for smoothness of working relationships with them.
11. Interdependence, accepts appropriate dependency needs of others as well as of him or herself.	Needs continuous direction and well-defined structure.	Can stand alone for a while, but needs to know higher authority is there to fall back on.	Insists on standing alone and denies need for others.	Cooperative, participative but doesn't move ahead of group. Can stand alone but not comfortable doing so.	Stands on own but invites information, criticism, and cooperation from others. Can yield temporarily to lead of more competent, specialized person without feeling loss of leadership role.
12. Articulateness, makes a good impression.	Clearly upset even when presenting reports in small meetings.	Can present reports but doesn't inspire excitement or confidence. Often displays nervous behavior.	Can make a decent presentation but it's hard work. Doesn't read audience well, seems somehow removed.	Handles him or herself well in public, but has difficulty dealing with hostile questions and unfriendly audiences.	Extremely presentable, has a wide-ranging vocabulary, inspires audience confidence, senses audience moods. Respected by peers for verbalizing and presenting their problems.

(continued)

Dimensions of leaders' personalities (continued)

13. Stamina, has physical as well as mental energy.	Low level of involvement and enthusiasm, so runs down fast.	Often starts projects energetically but doesn't maintain interest.	Can work through a significant problem at good energy level.	High level of energy. Requires normal battery recharging.	Consistent high energy level. Always at the ready. Doesn't seem to run out of steam, paces him- or herself well.
14. Adaptability, manages stress well.	Doesn't tolerate stress well. Many physical, personal, and family symptoms.	Can take stress if supported by others. Worries a lot about what might happen.	Does reasonably well under bursts of stress but not long, sustained pressures. Worries in a healthy way about solutions to problems.	Can take sustained pressure with normal symptoms. Has effective coping devices, such as consultation with others and taking time off.	Takes whatever comes down the pike and seems to thrive on it.
15. Sense of humor, doesn't take self too seriously.	Can't laugh at anything. Somber, forbidding, cold.	Can crack a smile once in a while. Humor limited to a few dimensions of behavior.	Laughs too easily at everything. Sometimes laughs inappropriately to ease own tension. Immature raconteur.	Occasional sparkle of wit. Not easily spontaneous but can laugh heartily at times. Has to work at telling a humorous story but is pleasant company.	Warm affectionate humor. Stories appropriate to place and position. Eases tensions naturally. Is welcome company.

16. Vision, is clear about progression of his or her own life and career, as well as where the organization should go.	Takes no interest in career, content to move along in the managerial current.	Has poorly defined, almost unrecognized, personal goals.	Broad goals, not clearly delineated, not necessarily related to organizational goals.	Well-defined goals, but behavior suggests that the personal agenda, for which organization is a device, is paramount.	Well-defined goals, consistent with organization's needs and values, constantly pursued.

17. Perseverance, able to stick to a task and see it through regardless of the difficulties encountered.	Loses interest fast.	Loses interest when encounters resistance or frustration.	Sustains interest as long as novelty or stimulation continues.	Sustains interest in face of discouragement, but gradually loses zest and optimism.	Keeps looking for ways around obstacles. Maintains optimism out of confidence a solution will be found.
18. Personal organization, has good sense of time.	Poorly organized; doesn't recognize priorities or keep track of information.	Organization and priorities erratic. Sometimes on top of things but easily thrown off.	Reasonably well-organized. Priorities sometimes questionable. Allows intrusion which eats time. Can answer questions but takes time to dig out information.	Well-organized. Can readily get information but doesn't have massive recall. Priorities appropriate. Governs own time.	Meticulously organized. Makes every minute count. Retrieves information readily, both from own head and organization.
19. Integrity, has a well-established value system, which has been tested in various ways in the past.	Chameleon. Can't really be trusted. Others' opinions have more weight than his or her own.	Variable. Usually responsible, but may give in under bottom-line pressure.	Ethical, but sometimes rationalizes decisions in favor of bottom line.	High standards. Struggles with ethical gray areas. Usually comes down on prudent side, doesn't shade decisions.	Beyond reproach, sometimes almost to point of rigidity.
20. Social responsibility, appreciates the need to assume leadership with respect to that responsibility.	No recognition of executive's public role or wish to fill it.	Recognizes public role but shies away from it. May veto ideas that might lead to taking it.	Recognizes role and wants to fill it out of obligation, but has no significant personal interest in it.	Recognizes executive responsibility and contributes, but in secondary roles.	Recognizes responsibility and relishes it as opportunity. Displays active leadership.

Notes

1. "A Politician-Turned Executive Surveys Both Worlds," *Fortune*, September 10, 1979, p. 88.

2. Roy Rowan, "Those Business Hunches Are More Than Blind Faith," *Fortune*, April 23, 1979, p. 111.

3. *New York Times*, July 15, 1979.

4. "A British Grant Goes Abroad for a Chief," *Business Week*, September 10, 1979, p. 102.

5. "The Singular Henry Singleton," *Forbes*, July 9, 1979, p. 45.

6. See Larry E. Greiner, "Evolution and Revolution as Organizations Grow," HBR July–August 1972, p. 37.

Reprint 80410

Originally published in July–August 1980

6
The Abrasive Personality

Not everyone who rises quickly in a company and has good analytical skills and a lot of energy is abrasive, nor are all abrasive people in high management levels, but when the two do coincide, top management has a real problem. The problem is simply how to keep the extraordinarily talented person in a position where he or she can be most effective, and at the same time not sacrifice the feelings and aspirations of the people who work with and for this person. According to this author, managers can cope with this dilemma by helping their abrasive subordinates to understand the negative consequences of their personalities. This method takes time and patience, but it is most likely the only way managers can save such people for the organization.

The corporate president stared out the window of his skyscraper office. His forehead was furrowed in anger and puzzlement. His fingers drummed the arm of his chair with a speed that signified intense frustration. The other executives in the room waited expectantly. Each had said his piece. Each had come to his and her own conclusion about the problem.

Darrel Sandstrom, vice president of one of the corporation's major divisions, was the problem. Sandstrom was one of those rare young men who had rocketed to the division vice presidency at an age when most of his peers were still in lower-middle management. "He is sharp," his peers said, "but watch out for his afterburn. You'll get singed as he goes by." And that, in a phrase, was the problem.

There was no question that Sandstrom was well on his way to the top. Others were already vying for a handhold on his coattails. He had a reputation for being a self-starter. Give him a tough problem, like a failing division, and he would turn it around almost before anyone knew what had happened. He was an executive who could quickly take charge, unerringly get to the heart of a problem, lay out the steps for overcoming it, bulldoze his way through corporate red tape, and reorganize to get the job done. All that was well and good. Unfortunately, that was not all there was to it.

In staff discussions and meetings with his peers Sandstrom would ask pointed questions and make incisive comments. However, he would also brush his peers' superfluous words aside with little tact, making them fearful to offer their thoughts in his presence. Often he would get his way in meetings because of the persuasiveness of his arguments and his commanding presentations, but just as often those who were responsible for following up the conclusions of a meeting would not do so.

In meetings with his superiors, his questions were appropriate, his conclusions correct, and his insights important assets in examining problems. But he would antagonize his superiors by showing little patience with points and questions that to him seemed irrelevant or elementary. Unwilling to compromise, Sandstrom was an intellectual bully with little regard for those of his colleagues who could not keep up with him.

There were complaints from subordinates too. Some resented his controlling manner. Fearing his wrath, they spoke up at meetings only when they knew it to be safe. They knew he would not accept mediocrity and so they strived to attain the perfection he demanded of them. When he said they had done a good job, they knew they had earned his compliments, though many felt he did not really mean what he said.

His meetings were not noted for their liveliness, in fact he did not have much of a sense of humor. On the golf course and tennis courts he was equally humorless and competitive. Playing as intensely as he worked, he did not know what a game was.

And now here he was. The division presidency was open and the corporate president was in a dilemma. To promote Sandstrom was to perpetuate in a more responsible position what seemed to many a combination of Moshe Dayan, General George Patton, and Admiral Hyman Rickover. Sandstrom would produce; no question about that. But at what cost? Could the corporation afford it? If Sandstrom did not get the job, the likelihood was that he would quit. The company could ill afford that either, for his division's bottom line was a significant portion of its bottom line.

Around the table the opinion was divided. "Fire him now," some said; "you'll have to do it sooner or later." "Be gentle with him," others said; "if you hurt him, he'll lose his momentum." "He'll mature with age," said others. Still others commented, "When he gets to be president, he'll relax." And there were those who said, "What difference does it make? He's bringing in the bucks." The corporate president faced the dilemma; Sandstrom could not be promoted but neither could he be spared. None of the options presented gave him a way out; none of them could.

Darrel Sandstrom epitomizes people who puzzle, dismay, frustrate, and enrage others in organizations—those who have an abrasive personality. Men and women of high, sometimes brilliant, achievement who stubbornly insist on having their own way and are contemptuous of others, are the bane of bosses, subordinates, peers, and colleagues.

In the long run, they are a bane to themselves as well; when they fail, their failure is usually due to their abrasive personalities. Because of their value to their organizations, however, their superiors frequently go to great lengths to help them fit in the organization. In fact, top executives probably refer more managers with abrasive personalities to psychologists and psychiatrists, and human relations training programs in order to rescue them, than any other single classification of executives.

In this article I describe the abrasive personality, trace its origins, and suggest what managers might do to both help and cope with such people.

A Profile

Like the proverbial porcupine, an abrasive person seems to have a natural knack for jabbing others in an irritating and sometimes painful way. But that knack masks a desperation worse than that of those who receive the jabs, namely, a need to be perfect. (For a closer look at how a need to be perfect drives a person to the point where he alienates and causes significant stress to most people around him, see the sidebar at the end of this article.) The person who becomes a Darrel Sandstrom however, is not just someone who needs perfection. He has other characteristics which, combined with that need, create the behavior others find so offensive.

Such a person is most usually extremely intelligent. With a passion for perfection, accuracy, and completeness, he pushes himself very hard and can be counted on to do a job well, often spectacularly. He tends to want to do the job himself, however, finding it difficult to lean on others who he feels will not do it to his standards, on time, or with the required finesse. He has, therefore, great difficulty delegating even $25 decisions. Such complete thoroughness, however, no matter how good for the company as a whole, tends to leave others figuratively breathless, making them feel that they cannot compete in the same league.

He is often keenly analytical, capable of cutting through to the nub of a problem, but with his need for constant achievement, he is impatient with those who cannot think as quickly or speak as forthrightly as he can. Thus his capacity for analysis tends not to be matched by equal skill as a leader to implement the answers he has deduced.

On a one-to-one basis he is often genial and helpful to people he is not supervising. But despite what he says, he is usually not a good developer of people for, frequently, they feel too inadequate when they have to compare themselves with him. Also, the abrasive person's intense rivalry with others often leads him to undercut them, even though he himself may not be aware of doing so.

When his competitive instincts overwhelm his judgment, an abrasive person will sometimes crudely raise issues others are reluctant to speak about, leaving himself a scapegoat for his own forthrightness. In groups he tends to dominate others, treating all differences as challenges to be debated and vanquished. At the same time that he is domineering to his subordinates, he is fawning to his superiors. If he feels himself to be exceptionally competent, however, he may try to dominate his superiors also.

Though often in imaginative pursuit of bigger and broader achievements for which he frequently gets many accolades, he may well leave his bosses and those around him with no sense of having any input to the task or project. He moves so fast and ranges so widely that even when he has good ideas, his boss will tend to turn him down fearing that if he gives an inch, the subordinate will take a mile. The boss feels there will be no catching him, no containing him, and no protecting the stellar subordinate, himself, or higher management from any waves that may be created, the backwash from which might overwhelm them all.

Once reined in by his boss, the abrasive person feels that he has been let down, that his efforts have been in vain. Feeling unjustly treated, he becomes angry because he was asked to do something and it did not end well. Therefore, he reasons, he is being penalized because other people are jealous, rivalrous, or do not want to undertake anything new. Seeing his boss as somebody to be outflanked, rather than as somebody whose step-by-step involvement is necessary for a project's success, he is politically insensitive and often righteously denies the need for such sensitivity.

Although others often perceive him as both grandiose and emotionally cold, the abrasive person has a strong and very intense emotional interest in himself. Needing to see himself as extraordinary, he acts sometimes as if he were a privileged person—indeed, as if he had a right to be different or even inconsiderate.

At times he sees others as mere devices for his self-aggrandizement, existing as extensions of himself, rather than as full-fledged, unique adults with their own wishes, desires, and aspirations. To inflate his always low sense of self-worth, he competes intensely for attention, affection, and applause. At the same time, he seems to expect others to accept his word, decision, or logic just because it is his. When disappointed in these expectations, he becomes enraged.

To such a person, self-control is very important, as is control of others, which he makes total if possible. Thus he overorganizes, and copes with imperfections in others by oversupervising them. To him, losing a little control is the same as losing total control. To prevent that, he is rigid, constricted, and unable to compromise. In fact, for him, making a compromise is the same as giving in to lower standards. He therefore has little capacity for the necessary give and take of organizational political systems. This inflexibility is especially apparent around issues of abstract values which, for him, become specifically concrete.

To others the same control makes him appear emphatically right, self-confident, and self-assured. In contrast, those who are not so sure of what they believe or of the clarity of an issue, feel inadequate and less virtuous.

The abrasive person, appearing to have encyclopedic knowledge, is often well read, and, with already a good academic background, strives for more. While subordinates and even peers may strive as well to meet the high expectations of such a person, and some may reach extraordinary heights, many ultimately give up, especially if he beats them down. Thus the legendary Vince Lombardi drove the Green Bay Packers to great success, but all of its members, recognizing that he was the key to their success, felt that the better and more competent he was the less adequate they were. When such a person dies or leaves an organization, those left behind are demoralized because they have no self-confidence. Usually they will feel that they have not been able to measure up and indeed, frequently, they cannot.

If they are compelled to retire, abrasive people will have difficulty. If they are not compelled to retire, they tend to hold on to the very end, and with age, their judgment is usually impaired. In their view, they have less and less need to adapt to people and circumstances, or to change their way of doing things. Thus they become more and more tangential to the main thrust of the business. If they are entrepreneurs, they may frequently destroy organizations in an unconscious effort to keep somebody else from taking over their babies. J. Edgar Hoover, a case in point, ultimately corrupted and very nearly destroyed the reputation of the FBI out of his own self-righteousness.

Solving the Dilemma

Given that you, the reader, have a subordinate who fits the profile I have drawn, what can you do? Corrective effort occurs in stages, and takes time and patience on everybody's part.

FIRST-STAGE TECHNIQUES

The following steps can be used with any employee who is having a behavior problem, but they are particularly effective in introducing an abrasive person to the consequences of his or her behavior.

- Recognize the psychological axiom that each person is always doing the best he can. Understanding that abrasive, provocative behavior springs from an extremely vulnerable self-image, a hunger for affection, and an eagerness for contact, do not become angry. Instead, initiate frequent discussion with this person.

- In such discussions, uncritically report your observations of his abrasive behavior. Describe what you see, especially the more subtle behavior to which people react automatically. Ask how he thinks others feel when he says or does what you describe. How does he think they are likely to respond? Is that the result he wants? If not, what would you do differently to get the response he wants? How would he respond if someone else said or did what he does?

- Point out that you recognize his desire to achieve and that you want to help. But tell him that if he wants to advance in the company, he needs to take others into account, and that his progress along these lines has implications for his future. Ensure him also that everyone experiences defeats and disappointments along the way.

- When, as is likely to be the case, his provocative behavior ultimately irritates you, try to avoid both impulsively attacking back on the one hand and being critical of yourself for not responding in kind on the other. Explain to him that although you understand his need to do or be the best, that he made you angry and that others he works with must feel the same. Tell him you get irritated and annoyed, particularly with hostile, depreciating, or controlling tactics. After all, you can say, you are only human, too, even if he thinks he is not. Let him know how frequently such behavior occurs.

- If he challenges, philosophizes, defends, or tries to debate your observations, or accuses you of hostility to him, do not counterattack. Tell him you are not interested in arguing. Merely report your observations of what he is doing or misinterpreting *at that moment*. Keep his goal the point of your discussion; does he want to make it or not?

- If your relationship is strong enough, you might ask why he must defend or attack in situations that are not combat. Point out that to be part of a critical examination of a problem is one thing; to turn such a situation into a win-lose argument is another.

- Expect to have to repeat this process again and again, pointing out legitimate achievements about which he can be proud. Explain that goals are achieved step by step, that compromise is not necessarily second best, that the all-or-none principle usually results in futile disappointment, and that perfection is not attainable.

Much good talent can be saved if managers employ these steps with their abrasive subordinates. Of course, some people are less abrasive than others and may be able to modulate their behavior voluntarily and cope consciously with their abrasive tendencies. For those who cannot, however, more drastic measures may be needed.

FURTHER STEPS

Sometimes people with unconscious drives cannot see reality despite repeated attempts to show them. Perhaps they are too busy thinking up defensive arguments or are preoccupied with their own thoughts. Whatever, if they do not respond to the gentle counseling I have described, then they should be confronted with what their arrogant, hostile, and controlling behavior is costing them.

Such people must be told *very early* on how their behavior undermines them. All too often afraid to do this, their bosses quickly become resentful and withdraw, leaving their subordinates uncomfortable, but not knowing why. Feeling anxious, the abrasive subordinate then attempts to win back the regard and esteem of the boss in the only way he knows, by intensifying this behavior. That only makes things worse.

Abrasive persons can make significant contributions to an organization, but managers need to steer them again and again into taking those political steps that will enable them to experience success rather than rejection. Rather than corral such people, who tend to figuratively butt their heads against restrictions, managers do better to act like sheepdogs, gently nudging them back into position when they stray.

Highly conscientious people, who need to demonstrate their own competence by doing things themselves, are likely to have had to prove themselves against considerable odds in the past. Their demonstration of competence has had to be in terms of what they, themselves, could do as individuals. Thus they need political guidance and instruction in teamwork, as well as support from a superior who will tell them the consequences of their behavior in straightforward terms.

These people will often need frequent feedback on each successive step they take in improving their political relationships. As they move slowly in such a process, or at least more slowly than they are accustomed to, they will experience increasing anxiety. While not demonstrating their individual competence, such people may feel that they are not doing well, and get so anxious that they may indeed fail. When they have such feelings, they then tend to revert to their old unilateral way of doing things.

However, if despite the boss's best efforts the subordinate does not respond, the manager must tell him *in no uncertain terms* that his behavior is abrasive and therefore unsatisfactory. Managers should not assume that their subordinates know this, but should tell them and tell them repeatedly, and in written form. Being told once or twice during a performance appraisal should be enough. My experience is, however, that most superiors are very reluctant to tell people, particularly abrasive ones, the effects of their behavior during performance appraisals.

In one instance, when I was asked to see such a manager, he did not know why he had been referred to me. When I told him, he was dismayed. Showing me his performance appraisal, he complained that his boss had not told him. Rather his boss had commented favorably on all his qualities and assets, and in one sentence had written that his behavior with people was improving. In reality, the boss was so enraged with his subordinate's behavior that he was not promoting him as far as he would have wished.

When the steps I have outlined have been followed to no avail, when the subordinate clearly knows, and he or she is unable to respond by changing his or her behavior, when repeated words to the person and even failures to be promoted have produced no significant improvement, there are two likely consequences. First, the abrasive person will feel unfairly treated, unrecognized for his or her skills and competence, and unappreciated for what he or she could bring to the organization. Second, the superior is usually desperate, angry, and at his wit's end.

If by this point the abrasive person has not already been referred to a competent psychologist or psychiatrist for therapy, he should be. *Nothing else will have a significant effect,* and even therapy may not. Whether it does will depend on the severity of the problem and the skill of the therapist. This is not a problem that will be solved in a T-group, or a weekend encounter, or some other form of confrontation.

The manager should make sure the subordinate understands that when a person is referred to a psychologist, there are two implications. The first is that the person is so competent, skilled, or capable in some dimension of his role that his superiors would not only hate to lose him, but also have reason to expect that the person could flower into a mature executive who can assume greater responsibility. The second is that despite his talent, the subordinate is so unable to get along with other people that he cannot be promoted beyond his present role. Both points should be made emphatically.

These same principles apply equally in dealing with any ineffective or dysfunctional behavior on the job. Some people cannot seem to get their work done. Others have a habit of getting in their own way as well as that of others. Still others manage to stumble their way to work

late each morning or produce incomplete or inadequate work. Whatever the case, steps in treating them are essentially the same.

Other Problem Situations

What do you do if the abrasive person is your boss, your peer, someone
you are interviewing, or, hardest to face of all, yourself? What recourse
do you have then?

THE BOSS

Let us assume that you are relatively new or inexperienced in a particular area and need a certain amount of time to achieve your own competence. Chances are that because of his knowledge and competence,
your abrasive boss will have much to teach. Since his high standards
will ensure that the model he provides will be a good one, there will be
sufficient reason for you to tolerate his abrasiveness.

But after two years, or whenever you establish your own competence, you will begin to chafe under the rigid control. As you push for
your own freedom, your boss is likely to become threatened with loss
of control and feel that you are becoming rivalrous. He is then likely to
turn on you, now no longer a disciple, and, in sometimes devious
ways, get back at you. Your memos will lie on his desk, unanswered.
Information being sent through channels will be delayed. Complaints,
suggestions, requests will either be rejected outright or merely tabled.
Sometimes he will reorganize the unit around you, which will fence
you in and force you to deal with decoys—nominal bosses who have
no real power.

If you are in a safe position, you might tell the boss how he appears
to you, and his effect on subordinates. If he is at a high level, it will
usually do little good to go above his head. Certainly, you should check
out how much concern his superiors have about him, how much they
are willing to tolerate, and how able they are to face him in a confrontation. Few at higher management levels are willing to take on a
bright, combative, seemingly self-confident opponent—especially if he
has a record of achievement, and there is little concrete evidence of the
negative effects of his behavior.

In short, after you have learned what you can from such a person, it
is probably time to get out from under him.

THE PEER

If you are the peer of an abrasive person, do not hesitate to tell him if his behavior intimidates you. Speaking of your irritation and anger and that of others, you might tell him you do not think he wants to deliberately estrange people or be self-defeating. He might become angry, but if approached in a kindly manner, he is more likely to be contrite and may even ask for more feedback on specific occasions.

THE CANDIDATE

What should you look for during an interview to avoid hiring someone who will turn out to be abrasive?

Pay attention to the charming personality. Not all charming persons are self-centered, but many are. Some preen themselves, dress to perfection, and in other ways indicate that they give an inordinate amount of attention to themselves. The more exhibitionistic the person, the more a person needs approval, the less he or she can be thoughtful of others. Also pay special attention to precision in speech or manner. Clarity is a virtue, but a need for exactness indicates a need to control.

Find out how the person gets things done by having him or her describe past projects and activities. How much does he report starting and finishing tasks all by himself, even to the surprise of his superiors? To do so is not necessarily bad; in fact, it may be good for a person to be a self-starter. But repeated singular achievement might indicate a problem in working as part of a team. How often does he use "I"? How closely did he have to check the work of subordinates? How important was it for him to have control of what was happening? How did he talk to people about their mistakes? How did he go about coaching them?

How did he view the limits and inadequacies of others, as human imperfections or as faults? How much better does he think things could have been done? Why were they not done better? Why could he not do better? What did his bosses say about him in performance appraisals?

YOU, YOURSELF

Finally, what if you are abrasive? If you ask yourself the questions in the sidebar at the end of this article, "Do You Have an Abrasive

Personality?" and find that you answer three of them in the affirmative, the chances are that your behavior is abrasive to the people around you. If you answer six or more affirmatively, it takes no great insight to recognize that you have more problems than are good for your career. Of course, none of these questions taken by itself is necessarily indicative of anything, but enough affirmative answers may reveal an abrasive profile.

If you are the problem and it troubles you, you can work at self-correction. Most often, however, you need the help of a third person—your spouse, a friend, your boss, or a professional. If your behavior causes you serious problems on the job, then a professional is indicated. Managers and executives with naturally heavy orientations to control, need to check themselves carefully for this kind of behavior lest unconsciously they defeat their own ends.

The Need to Be Perfect

If a person's ultimate aspiration, his ego ideal, is perfection, then he is always going to fall short of it—by astronomical distances. And if this person's self-image is already low, the distance between where he perceives himself to be and the omnipotence he wants to attain will be constantly increasing as the feeling of failure continues. He must, therefore, push himself ever harder—all the time. Others who are or may be viewed as competitors threaten his self-image even further; if they win, by his own definition, he loses. His intense need to be perfect then becomes translated into intense rivalry.

If a person is always pushing himself toward impossible aspirations and is never able to achieve them, there are two consequences for his emotions. The greater the gap between his ego ideal and self-image, the greater will be both his guilt and anger with himself for not achieving the dream. And the angrier a person is with himself the more likely he is to attack himself or drive himself to narrow the gap between his ideal and his present self-image. Only in narrowing the gap can he reduce his feelings of anger, depression, and inadequacy.

However, as the unconscious drive for perfection is irrational, no degree of conscious effort can possibly achieve the ideal nor decrease the self-punishment such a person brings down on himself for not achieving it. The anger and self-hatred are never ending, therefore, and build up to the point where they spill over in the form of hostile attacks on peers and subordinates, such as treating them with contempt and condescension.

These feelings may also spill over onto spouses, children, and even pets. In fact, the abrasive person's need for self-punishment may also be so great that he may take great, albeit neurotic, pleasure provoking others who will subsequently reject, that is, punish him. In effect, he acts as if he were his own parent, punishing himself as well as others. In Anna Freud's words, he becomes a good hater.[1]

---

1. Anna Freud, "Comments on Aggression," International Journal of Psychoanalysis, *vol. 53, no. 2, 1972,* p. 163.

Do You Have an Abrasive Personality?

You might ask yourself these questions. Then ask them of your spouse, your peers, your friends—and even your subordinates:

1. Are you condescendingly critical? When you talk of others in the organization, do you speak of "straightening them out" or "whipping them into shape"?
2. Do you need to be in full control? Does almost everything need to be cleared with you?
3. In meetings, do your comments take a disproportionate amount of time?
4. Are you quick to rise to the attack, to challenge?
5. Do you have a need to debate? Do discussions quickly become arguments?
6. Are people reluctant to discuss things with you? Does no one speak up? When someone does, are his or her statements inane?
7. Are you preoccupied with acquiring symbols of status and power?
8. Do you weasel out of responsibilities?
9. Are you reluctant to let others have the same privileges or perquisites as yourself?
10. When you talk about your activities, do you use the word "I" disproportionately?
11. Do your subordinates admire you because you are so strong and capable or because, in your organization, they feel so strong and capable—and supported?
12. To your amazement, do people speak of you as cold and distant when you really want them to like you?
13. Do you regard yourself as more competent than your peers, than your boss? Does your behavior let them know that?

Reprint 78307

Originally published in May–June 1978

7
Appraisal of *What* Performance?

It may be stretching it a bit to argue that the epigram "It's not the winning or losing that counts, but how you play the game" ought to be strictly followed in designing performance appraisal systems. In business, results are important, and few would disagree. What the epigram points out, however, is that some results are not worth the means some take to achieve them. Nonetheless, most performance systems in most companies focus on results of behavior while in reality people are judged just as much on how they get things done. In this article, the author argues that in order for a company to have a performance appraisal system that accounts for the "how" as well as the "what," it will need to establish: job descriptions that are behavior- as well as results-oriented; a critical incident program in which managers write reports regularly on the behavior of their employees; and support mechanisms to help managers honestly appraise the behavior of their employees as well as of their bosses.

A corporate president put a senior executive in charge of a failing operation. His only directive was "Get it in the black." Within two years of that injunction, the new executive moved the operation from a deficit position to one that showed a profit of several million. Fresh from his triumph, the executive announced himself as a candidate for a higher-level position, and indicated that he was already receiving offers from other companies.

The corporate president, however, did not share the executive's positive opinions of his behavior. In fact, the president was not at all pleased with the way the executive had handled things.

Naturally the executive was dismayed, and when he asked what he had done wrong, the corporate president told him that he had indeed accomplished what he had been asked to do, but he had done it single-handedly, by the sheer force of his own personality. Furthermore, the executive was told, he had replaced people whom the company thought to be good employees with those it regarded as compliant. In effect, by demonstrating his own strength, he had made the organization weaker. Until the executive changed his authoritarian manner, his boss said, it was unlikely that he would be promoted further.

Implicit in this vignette is the major fault in performance appraisal and management by objectives—namely, a fundamental misconception of what is to be appraised.

Performance appraisal has three basic functions: (1) to provide adequate feedback to each person on his or her performance; (2) to serve as a basis for modifying or changing behavior toward more effective working habits; and (3) to provide data to managers with which they may judge future job assignments and compensation. The performance appraisal concept is central to effective management. Much hard and imaginative work has gone into developing and refining it. In fact, there is a great deal of evidence to indicate how useful and effective performance appraisal is. Yet present systems of performance appraisal do not serve any of these functions well.

As it is customarily defined and used, performance appraisal focuses not on behavior but on outcomes of behavior. But even though the executive in the example achieved his objective, he was evaluated on *how* he attained it. Thus, while the system purports to appraise results, in practice, people are really appraised on how they do things—which is not formally described in the setting of objectives, and for which there are rarely data on record.

In my experience, the crucial aspect of any manager's job and the source of most failures, which is practically never described, is the "how." As long as managers appraise the ends yet actually give greater weight to the means, employ a static job description base which does not describe the "how," and do not have support mechanisms for the appraisal process, widespread dissatisfaction with performance appraisal is bound to continue. In fact, one personnel authority speaks of performance appraisal as "the Achilles heel of our profession . . ."[1]

Just how these inadequacies affect performance appraisal systems and how they can be corrected to provide managers with realistic bases for making judgments about employees' performance is the subject of this article.

Inadequacies of Appraisal Systems

It is widely recognized that there are many things inherently wrong with most of the performance appraisal systems in use. The most obvious drawbacks are:

- No matter how well defined the dimensions for appraising performance on quantitative goals are, judgments on performance are usually subjective and impressionistic.
- Because appraisals provide inadequate information about the subtleties of performance, managers using them to compare employees for the purposes of determining salary increases often make arbitrary judgments.
- Ratings by different managers, and especially those in different units, are usually incomparable. What is excellent work in one unit may be unacceptable in another in the same company.
- When salary increases are allocated on the basis of a curve of normal distribution, which is in turn based on rating of results rather than on behavior, competent employees may not only be denied increases, but may also become demotivated.[2]
- Trying to base promotion and layoff decisions on appraisal data leaves the decisions open to acrimonious debate. When employees who have been retired early have complained to federal authorities of age discrimination, defendant companies have discovered that there were inadequate data to support the layoff decisions.
- Although managers are urged to give feedback freely and often, there are no built-in mechanisms for ensuring that they do so. Delay in feedback creates both frustration, when good performance is not quickly recognized, and anger, when judgment is rendered for inadequacies long past.
- There are few effective established mechanisms to cope with either the sense of inadequacy managers have about appraising subordinates, or the paralysis and procrastination that result from guilt about playing God.

Some people might argue that these problems are deficiencies of managers, not of the system. But even if that were altogether true, managers are part of that system. Performance appraisal needs to be viewed not as a technique but as a process involving both people and data, and as such the whole process is inadequate.

Recognizing that there are many deficiencies in performance appraisals, managers in many companies do not want to do them. In

other companies there is a great reluctance to do them straightfor-
wardly. Personnel specialists attribute these problems to the reluctance
of managers to adopt new ways and to the fear of irreparably damaging
their subordinates' self-esteem. In government, performance appraisal
is largely a joke, and in both private and public enterprise, merit ratings
are hollow.[3]

One of the main sources of trouble with performance appraisal systems is, as I have already pointed out, that the outcome of behavior
rather than the behavior itself is what is evaluated. In fact, most
people's jobs are described in terms that are only quantitatively measurable; the job description itself is the root of the problem.

The Static Job Description

When people write their own job descriptions (or make statements
from which others will write them) essentially they define their
responsibilities and basic functions. Then on performance appraisal
forms, managers comment on these functions by describing what an
individual is supposed to accomplish. Forms in use in many companies
today have such directions as:

1. "List the major objectives of this person's job that can be measured
   qualitatively or quantitatively."
2. "Define the results expected and the standards of performance—
   money, quantity, quality, time limits, or completion dates."
3. "Describe the action planned as a result of this appraisal, the next
   steps to be taken—reevaluation, strategy, tactics, and so on."
4. "List the person's strong points—his assets and accomplishments—
   and his weak points—areas in which improvement is needed. What
   are the action plans for improvement?"

In most instances the appraiser is asked to do an overall rating with a
five point scale or some similar device. Finally, he is asked to make a
statement about the person's potential for the next step or even for
higher-level management.

Nowhere in this set of questions or in any of the performance
appraisal systems I have examined is anything asked about *how* the
person is to attain the ends he or she is charged with reaching.

While some may assert that the ideal way of managing is to give a
person a charge and leave him or her alone to accomplish it, this principle is oversimplified both in theory and practice. People need to

know the topography of the land they are expected to cross, and the routes as perceived by those to whom they report.

Every manager has multiple obligations, not the least of which are certain kinds of relationships with peers, subordinates, and various consumer, financial, government, supplier, and other publics. Some of these are more important than others, and some need to be handled with much greater skill and aplomb than others. In some situations a manager may be expected to take a vigorous and firm stand, as in labor negotiations; in others he may have to be conciliative; in still others he may even have to be passive. Unless these varied modes of expected behavior are laid out, the job description is static. Because static job descriptions define behavior in gross terms, crucially important differentiated aspects of behavior are lost when performance appraisals are made.

For example, in one of the more progressive performance appraisal systems, which is used by an innovative company, a manager working out his own job description prepares a mission or role statement of what he is supposed to do according to the guide which specifically directs him to concentrate on the what and the when, not on the why and the how.[4] The guide instructs him to divide his mission into four general areas: (1) innovation, (2) problem solving, (3) ongoing administration, and (4) personal.

In still another company, a manager appraising a subordinate's performance is asked to describe an employee's accomplishments, neglected areas, goals, and objectives. The manager is told that he is to recognize good work, suggest improvement, get agreement on top priority elements of the task, clarify responsibility, verify and correct rumors, and talk about personal and long-range goals.

In another company's outstanding performance appraisal guide, which reflects great detail and careful consideration, the categories are: work, effectiveness with others, problem solving, decision making, goal setting, organizing and planning, developing subordinates, attending to self-development, and finding initiatives. Each of these categories is broken down into example statements such as: "exhibits high level of independence in work"; "identifies problems and deals with them"; "appropriately subordinates departmental interest to overall company goal"; or "gives people genuine responsibility, holds them accountable, and allows them freedom to act."

Some personnel researchers have advocated role analysis techniques to cope with static job descriptions, and this is a step in the right direction.[5]

But even these techniques are limited because they lean heavily on what other people—supervisors, subordinates, peers—expect of the manager. These expectations are also generalized; they do not specify behavior.

Nowhere in these examples is an individual told what *behavior* is expected of him in a range of contexts. Who are the sensitive people with whom certain kinds of relationships have to be maintained? What are the specific problems and barriers? What have been the historic manufacturing blunders or frictions? How should union relationships and union leaders be dealt with? What are the specific integrative problems to be resolved and what are the historical conflicts? These and many more similar pieces of behavior will be the true bases on which a person will be judged, regardless of the questions an appraisal form asks.

Static job descriptions are catastrophic for managers. Job proficiency and goal achievement usually are necessary but not sufficient conditions for advancement; the key elements in whether one makes it in an organization are political. The collective judgments made about a person, which rarely find their way into performance appraisals, become the social web in which he or she must live. Therefore, when a person is placed in a new situation, whether in a different geographical site, at a different level in the hierarchy, or in a new role, he must be apprised of the subtleties of the relationships he will have with those who will influence his role and his career. Furthermore, he must be helped to differentiate the varied kinds of behavior required to succeed.

Some people develop political diagnostic skill very rapidly; often, however, these are people whose social senses enable them to move beyond their technical and managerial competence. And some may be out and out manipulative charlatans who succeed in business without really trying, and whose promotion demoralizes good people. But the great majority of people, those who have concentrated heavily on their professional competence at the expense of acquiring political skill early, will need to have that skill developed, ideally by their own seniors. That development process requires: (1) a dynamic job description, (2) a critical incident process, and (3) a psychological support system.

Dynamic Job Description

If a static job description is at the root of the inadequacies of performance appraisal systems, what is needed is a different kind of job description. What we are looking for is one that amplifies statements of job responsibility and desired outcome by describing the emotional and behavioral topography of the task to be done by the individual in the job.

Psychologists describe behavior in many ways, each having his or her own preferences. I have found four major features of behavior to be fundamentally important in a wide range of managerial settings. These features have to do with how a person characteristically manages what some psychologists call aggression, affection, dependency, and also the nature of the person's ego ideal.[6]

Using his preferred system, one can begin formulating a dynamic job description by describing the characteristic behavior required by a job. This is what these terms mean with respect to job descriptions:

1. *How does this job require the incumbent to handle his aggression, his attacking capacity?* Must he or she vanquish customers? Must he hold on to his anger in the face of repeated complaints and attacks from others? Will she be the target of hostility and, if so, from whom? Must he give firm direction to others? Must she attack problems vigorously, but handle some areas with great delicacy and finesse? Which problems are to be attacked with vigor and immediacy and which coolly and analytically?

2. *How does this job require the incumbent to manage affection, the need to love and to be loved?* Is the person required to be a socially friendly leader of a close-knit work group? Should the person work closely and supportively with subordinates for task accomplishment? Is the task one in which the person will have to be content with the feeling of a job well done, or is it one which involves more public display and recognition? Will he be obscure and unnoticed, or highly visible? Must she lavish attention on the work, a product, a service, or customers? Must he be cold and distant from others and, if so, from whom?

3. *How does this job require the incumbent to manage dependency needs?* Will the individual be able to lean on others who have skill and competencies, or will he have to do things himself? How much will she be on her own and in what areas? How much support will there be from superiors and staff functions? How well defined is the nature of the work? What kind of feedback provisions are there? What are the structural and hierarchical relationships? How solid

are they and to whom will the person turn and for what? With which people must he interact in order to accomplish what he needs to accomplish, and in what manner?

4. *What ego ideal demands does this job fulfill?* If one does the task well, what are the gratifications to be gained? Will the person make a lot of money? Will he achieve considerable organizational and public recognition? Will she be eligible for promotion? Will he feel good about himself and, if so, in what ways? Why? Will she acquire a significant skill, an important element of reputation, or an organizational constituency? Will he acquire power?

Individuals may be described along the same four dynamic dimensions: How does this person characteristically handle aggression? How does he or she characteristically handle affection? How does he or she characteristically handle dependency needs? What is the nature of his or her ego ideal?

Once the subtleties of the task are defined and individuals described, people may be matched to tasks. I am not advocating a return to evaluation of personality traits. I am arguing for more dynamic conception of the managerial role and a more dynamic assessment of an employee's characteristics. And only when a person's behavior is recognized as basic to how he performs his job will performance appraisal systems be realistic.

Critical Incident Process

Having established a dynamic job description for a person, the next step is to evolve a complementary performance appraisal system that will provide feedback on verifiable behavior, do so in a continuous fashion, and serve coaching-, promotion-, and salary-data needs.

Ideally, a manager and his subordinate will have defined together the objectives to be attained in a certain job, and the criteria by which each will know that those objectives have been attained, including the more qualitative aspects of the job. Then they will have spelled out the subtleties of how various aspects of the job must be performed. They will in this way have elaborated the *behavioral* requirements of the task.

In order for performance appraisal to be effective for coaching, teaching, and changing those aspects of an employee's behavior that are amenable to change, an employee needs to know about each piece of behavior that is good, as well as that which for some reason is not acceptable or needs modification. Such incidents will occur randomly and be judged randomly by his manager.

So that there will be useful data, the manager needs to quickly write down what he has said to the subordinate, describing in a paragraph what the subordinate did or did not do, in what setting, under what circumstances, about what problem. This information forms a *behavioral* record, a critical incident report of which the subordinate already has been informed and which is now in his folder, open to his review. Examples of two incidents can be found in the sidebar "Examples of Critical Incidents" at the end of this article.

This critical incident technique is not new.[7] In the past it has been used largely for case illustrations and, in modified forms, has been suggested as a method for first-level supervisors to evaluate line employees. Supervisors already record negative incidents concerning line employees because warnings and disciplinary steps must be documented. However, efforts to develop scales from critical incidents for rating behavior have not worked well.[8] Behavior is too complex to be scaled along a few dimensions and then rated.

But instead of scaling behavior, one might directly record the behavior of those being appraised, and evaluate it at a later date. There are other good reasons for adopting this technique as well. At last, here is a process that provides data to help managers perform the basic functions of performance appraisal systems—namely, provide feedback, coaching, and promotion data. Another plus is that recorded data live longer than the manager recording them.

Here is how behavioral data might be put to use in the critical incident process:

1. *Feedback data.* When there is a semiannual or annual review, an employee will have no surprises and the manager will have on paper what he is using as a basis for making his summary feedback and appraisal. Because the data are on record, an employee cannot deny having heard what was said earlier, nor must the manager try to remember all year what have been the bases of his judgments.

   Also, as each critical incident is recorded, over time there will be data in an individual's folder to be referred to when and if there are suits alleging discrimination. Critical incidents of behavior, which illustrate behavior patterns, will be the only hard evidence acceptable to adjudicating bodies.

2. *Coaching data.* When employees receive feedback information at the time the incident occurs, they may be able to adapt their behavior more easily. With this technique, the employee will receive indications more often on how he is doing, and will be able to correct small problems before they become large ones. Also, if the employee cannot change his behavior, that fact will become evident to him through the repetitive critical incident notes. If the employee feels unfairly judged or criticized, he may appeal immediately rather than long after the fact. If there are few or no incidents on record, that in itself says something about job behavior, and may be used as a basis for discussion. In any event, both manager and employee will know which behavior is being appraised.

3. *Promotion data.* With such an accumulation of critical incidents, a manager or the personnel department is in a position to evaluate repeatedly how the person characteristically manages aggression, affection, and dependency needs, and the nature of his ego ideal. These successive judgments become cumulative data for better job fit.

When a person is provided continuously with verifiable information, including when he has been passed over for promotion and why, he is able to perceive more accurately the nuances of his behavior and his behavioral patterns. Thus, when offered other opportunities, the employee is in a better position to weigh his own behavioral configurations against those required by the prospective job. A person who knows himself in this way will be more easily able to say about a given job, "That's not for me." He will see that the next job in the pyramid is not necessarily rightfully his. In recognizing his own behavioral limitations he may save himself much grief as well as avoid painful difficulty for his superiors and the organization.

But the most important reason for having such information is to increase the chances of success of those who are chosen for greater responsibility. In most personnel folders there is practically no information about how a manager is likely to do when placed on his own. Data about dependency are noticeably absent, and many a shining prospect dims when there is no one to support him in a higher-level job. Managements need to know early on who can stand alone, and they cannot know that without behavioral information.

4. *Long-term data.* Frequently, new managers do not know their employees and all too often have little information in the folder with which to appraise them. This problem is compounded when managers move quickly from one area to another. For his part, the employee just as frequently has to prove himself to transient bosses who hold his fate in their hands but know nothing of his past performance. With little information, managers feel unqualified to make judgments. With the critical incident process, however, managers can report incidents which can be summarized by someone else.

Some may object to "keeping book" on their people or resist a program of constant reviews and endless reports—both extreme views. Some may argue that supervisors will not follow the method. But if managers cannot get raises for or transfer employees without adequate documentation, they will soon learn the need to follow through. The critical incident process compels superiors to face subordinates, a responsibility too many shirk.

While it might seem difficult to analyze performance in terms of aggression, affection, dependency, the ego ideal, or other psychological concepts, to do so is no different from learning to use economic, financial, or accounting concepts. Many managers already talk about these same issues in other words, for example: "taking charge" versus "being a nice guy"; "needing to be stroked" versus the "self-starter"; "fast track" versus the "shelf-sitter." A little practice, together with support mechanisms, can go a long way.

Support Mechanisms

Performance appraisal cannot be limited to a yearly downward reward-punishment judgment. Ideally, appraisal should be a part of a continuing process by which both manager and employee may be guided. In addition, it should enhance an effective superior-subordinate relationship.

To accomplish these aims, performance appraisal must be supported by mechanisms that enable the manager to master his inadequacies and to cope with his feelings of guilt; have a record of that part of his work that occurs outside the purview of his own boss (e.g., task force assignments which require someone to appraise a whole group); and modify those aspects of his superior's behavior which hamper his performance. All of this requires an upward appraisal process.

1. *Managing the guilt.* The manager's guilt about appraising subordinates appears when managers complain about playing God, about destroying people. A great crippler of effective performance appraisal is the feeling of guilt, much of which is irrational, but which most people have when they criticize others.[9] Guilt is what leads to the fear of doing appraisals. It is the root of procrastination, of the failure to appraise honestly, and of the overreaction which can demolish subordinates.

   Fortunately, there are group methods for relieving guilt and for helping managers and supervisors understand that critical importance, indeed the necessity, of accurate behavioral evaluations. One way is by having people together at the same peer level discuss their problems in appraisal and talk about their feelings in undertaking the appraisal task. In addition, rehearsals of role playing increase a manager's sense of familiarity and competence and ease his anxiety.

   In fact, a five-step process, one step per week for five weeks, can be extremely helpful:

   - Week one: Group discussion among peers (no more than 12) about their feelings about appraising subordinates.
   - Week two: Group discussions resulting in advice from each other on the specific problems that each anticipates in appraising individuals.
   - Week three: Role playing appraisal interviews.
   - Week four: Actual appraisals.
   - Week five: Group discussion to review the appraisals, problems encountered, both anticipated and unanticipated, lessons learned, and skill needs that may have surfaced.

2. *Group appraisal.* By group appraisal, I do not mean peer approval of each other, which usually fails; rather, I mean appraisal of a group's accomplishment. When people work together in a group, whether reporting to the same person or not, they need to establish criteria by which they and those to whom they report will know how well

the task force or the group has done—in terms of behavior as well as results. Group appraisals provide information that is helpful both in establishing criteria as well as in providing each individual with feedback.

At the end of a given task, a group may do a group appraisal or be appraised by the manager to whom they report, and that appraisal may be entered into folders of each of the people who are involved. It will then serve as another basis for managerial- and self-judgment.

3. *Upward appraisal.* Finally, there should be upward appraisal. Some beginning voluntary steps in this direction are being taken in the Sun Oil Company, and by individual executives in other companies. Upward appraisal is a very difficult process because most managers do not want to be evaluated by their subordinates. As a matter of fact, however, most managers *are* evaluated indirectly by their employees, and these evaluations are frequently behavioral.

The employees' work itself is a kind of evaluation. Their work may be done erratically or irresponsibly. Or they may be poorly motivated. Negative behavior is a form of appraisal, and one from which a manager gains little. A manager cannot be quite sure what precipitated the behavior he sees, let alone be sure what to do about it.

If, however, the manager is getting dynamic behavioral appraisal from his employees, then he, too, may correct his course. But if he asks his subordinates for upward appraisal without warning, he is likely to be greeted with dead silence and great caution. A helpful way to deal with this situation is to ask one's employees to define the criteria by which they would appraise the manager's job, not to judge his actual performance.

This process of definition may require a manager to meet with employees weekly for months to define the criteria. By the end of three months, say, the employees should be much more comfortable working with their manager on this issue. And if the manager can be trusted at all, then when he or she finally asks them to evaluate the performance, including specific behaviors, along the dimensions they have worked out together, they are likely to be more willing to do so. Of course, if there is no trust, there is no possibility of upward appraisal. In any event, the upward performance appraisal should go to the manager's superior so that people do not jeopardize themselves by speaking directly.

Under present performance appraisal systems, it is difficult to compensate managers for developing people because the criteria are elusive. With a developing file of upward appraisals, however, executives can judge how well a manager has done in developing his people. The employees cannot evaluate the whole of their manager's job, but they can say a great deal about how well he or she has facilitated their work, increased their proficiency, cleared barriers, protected them against political forces, and raised their level of competence—in short, how the manager has met their ministration, maturation, and mastery needs.[10] A top executive can then quantify such upward evaluations and use the outcome as a basis for compensating a manager for his effectiveness in developing his employees.

When a group of manager peers experiments with upward appraisal and works it out to their own comfort, as well as to that of their employees, then it might be tried at the next lower level. When several successive levels have worked out their own systems, the process might be formalized throughout the organization. Acceptance of the upward appraisal concept is likely to be greater if it has been tested and modeled by the very people who must use it, and if it has not been imposed on them by the personnel department. With appropriate experience, the managers involved in the process would ultimately evolve suitable appraisal forms.

What About Results?

What does adopting the critical incident technique and the dynamic job description mean for judging a person's ability to obtain results? Does quantitative performance lose its importance?

My answer is an unqualified no. There will always be other issues that managers will have to determine, such as level of compensation or promotability—issues which should be dealt with in other sessions after the basic behavioral performance appraisal.[11]

Some of the performance appraisal information may be helpful in making such determinations, but neither of these two functions should contaminate the performance appraisal feedback process. There can still be an annual compensation evaluation, based not only on behavior, which is the basis for coaching, but also on outcome. Did an employee make money? Did he reach quantitative goals? Did she resolve problems in the organization that were her responsibility?

No doubt, there will be some overlapping between behavior and outcome, but the two are qualitatively different. One might behave as it was expected he should, but at the same time not do what had to be done to handle the vagaries of the marketplace. He might not have responded with enough speed or flexibility to a problem, even though his behavior corresponded to all that originally was asked of him in the job description and goal-setting process.

Both behavior and outcome are important, and neither should be overlooked. It is most important, however, that they not be confused.

Examples of Critical Incidents

On May 15, the director of manufacturing, together with the president of the union, met with a group of shop stewards and the international business agent who were irate about the temporary 10% cutback in working hours. The cutback had been prematurely announced by corporate personnel without local consultation. The director of manufacturing heard them out, did not get hot under the collar about their tirade, and then explained the need to use up inventories. By reassuring them of the company's true intention, the director of manufacturing reduced tension in the plants.

—Executive Vice President

The director of manufacturing and I met today (August 13th) to review his development plans for his subordinates. While these are broadly defined on paper, the director does not hear enough from his subordinates about *their* objectives or ask enough about what *they* are up against. He is impatient with this aspect of his responsibility. I suggested that he allot regular meeting times for such discussions and take more time to listen. He agreed to do so.

—Executive Vice President

Notes

1. Herbert Heneman, "Research Roundup," *The Personnel Administrator,* June 1975, p. 61.

2. Paul H. Thompson and Gene W. Dalton, "Performance Appraisal: Managers Beware," HBR January–February 1970, p. 149.

3. Herbert S. Meyer, "The Pay for Performance Dilemma," *Organizational Dynamics,* Winter 1975, p. 39.

4. John B. Lasagna, "Make Your MBO Pragmatic," HBR November–December 1971, p. 64.

5. Ishwar Dayal, "Role Analysis Techniques in Job Descriptions," *California Management Review,* Summer 1969, p. 47.

6. Harry Levinson, *The Great Jackass Fallacy* (Cambridge: Harvard University Press, 1973), Ch. 3.

7. John C. Flanagan, "The Critical Incident Technique," *Psychological Bulletin,* 51:327, 1954, and John C. Flanagan (coauthor Robert K. Burns), "The Employee Performance Record: A New Appraisal and Development Tool," HBR September–October 1955, p. 95.

8. Donald P. Schwab, Herbert G. Heneman III, and Thomas A. DeCotis, "Behaviorally Anchored Rating Scales: A Review of the Literature," *Personnel Psychology,* 28:549, 1975.

9. Harry Levinson, "Management By Whose Objectives," HBR July–August 1970, p. 125.

10. Harry Levinson, *The Exceptional Executive* (Cambridge: Harvard University Press, 1968).

11. Herbert H. Meyer, Emanual Kay, and John R.P. French, Jr., "Split Roles in Performance Appraisal," HBR January–February 1965, p. 123.

Reprint 76405

Originally published in July–August 1976

8
Asinine Attitudes Toward Motivation

What this noted psychologist calls "the great jackass fallacy" is an unconscious managerial assumption about people and how they should be motivated. It results in the powerful treating the powerless as objects and in the perpetuation of anachronistic organizational structures that destroy the individual's sense of worth and accomplishment. And it is responsible for the "motivational crisis" that afflicts many large organizations. The author argues that in today's climate of increased pressure on organizations to become more responsive to both their members and society, it is particularly incumbent on managers to recognize the effect of the jackass fallacy on their thinking and to counter its effects on their organizations. Then he offers some suggestions for taking the first steps in this direction.

In spite of the corporate efforts to promote smooth management-employee relations, events like these continue to happen:

- The top management of a large manufacturing company discovers that some of its line employees have embezzled a five-figure sum while their supervisors stood by unperturbed. The executives are dumbfounded. They had thought that the supervisors were loyal, and that they themselves were thoughtful and kindly.

- An airline purchases a fleet of hydraulic lift trucks for placing food aboard aircraft at a large New York terminal. Although these trucks cost hundreds of thousands of dollars, they sit disabled on the airport apron. Maintenance employees and technicians occasionally glance at them contemptuously as they go about their work in sullen anger. Management is dismayed that these employees seem unresponsive to its cost-reduction efforts.

- Large companies, seeking new products, acquire smaller companies. Almost invariably, the successful managements of the acquired companies are soon gone and no new products are forthcoming. The larger organizations only increase their size and managerial burdens, and the hoped-for advantages evaporate. While this happens repeatedly, executives do not seem to learn from such failures.

When these events are looked at psychologically, their underlying causes become evident.

In the *first case,* the manufacturer renegotiated its labor contract every two years. Obviously, the appropriate person to do so was the vice president in charge of labor relations. But the people who carried out the contract and knew the employees best were the first-level supervisors; no one asked them what should be in the contract and what problems they had in implementing it. By its actions, management communicated to the supervisors that they did not matter much.

Furthermore, the union let grievances pile up just before the contract came up for renewal every two years, knowing full well that, to get a contract, management would settle the grievances in the union's favor. But the supervisors were the ones who bore the brunt of the grievances, since they carried out the terms of the contract. When management gave in, the supervisors felt that they had been undercut. In effect, these people were being told that they were stupid, that they had nothing useful to contribute to policy making, and that their job was to do as they were told. So they stood by during the stealing—if management did not care about them, why should they care about management?

In the *second case,* the issue for the airlines was much the same. A purchasing officer had bought the trucks, complete with sophisticated electronic controls. What was more natural than the purchasing officer doing the buying and getting the best? But he failed to check with the mechanics and technicians who kept the trucks operating. After all, what did they know about buying, and who asks technicians anyway?

Had he asked them, he would have learned that sophisticated electronic controls were fine for Los Angeles and Phoenix, where the weather was dry and mild, but that they failed repeatedly in New York, where the trucks were exposed to variable and sometimes harsh weather. No matter how hard the technicians worked, they could not keep the trucks functioning. Like the supervisors in the previous example, they felt that they were being exploited and contemptuously treated. Ultimately, they gave up trying to keep the trucks going. See-ing how much money the company had wasted on the trucks, they had little incentive to economize in their own small ways.

In the *third case,* what happens most frequently in merger failures is that the parent (note the use of that word) company promises the newly acquired company that there will be no changes. But changes are soon forthcoming, and the first of these is likely to be in the area of accounting control systems. Obviously, controls are necessary, and, just as obviously, many small companies do not have sophisticated con-trols. But they tend to be flexibly innovative for that specific reason. When controls become the central thrust of management, creative people who need flexibility leave, and the parent company is left with a corporate shell. The communication to the acquired company is that it is stupid and unsophisticated and therefore the parent must control it more rigidly.

Each of the foregoing problems would be dismissed in most organi-zations simply as a "failure in communications." Many psychologists would advocate dealing with such difficulties by participative manage-ment. Yet beneath that glib "explanation," and unresponsive to that ready "remedy," lies a fundamental unconscious management attitude that is responsible for most contemporary management-labor prob-lems and for what is now being called a "crisis in motivation." I call this attitude the great jackass fallacy.

Later in this article, I shall describe the fallacy in detail and offer some suggestions for correcting it. But first let us explore in more depth the motivational crisis that it has precipitated.

Motivational Miasma

The crisis takes many forms, and its effects are easy to spot. Here are just a few examples:

- Companies are repeatedly reorganized on the advice of management consultants, but to little avail in the long run.
- New managerial devices, such as the four-day workweek and putting hourly people on salary, are loudly touted for their effect on employee motivation and morale, but the old problems soon reappear.
- Efforts to enrich jobs by giving employees more responsibility show encouraging results, but these disappear when employees seek to influ-ence company policy and then are turned down by management.

- Business and nonprofit organizations alike are burdened by job encumbrances that result from union-management compromises.
- Increasing numbers of middle managers, engineers, teachers, and hospital personnel turn toward unionization.
- Many people in managerial ranks resign in favor of new jobs that pay less but offer greater individual freedom and initiative.

Most executives with whom I come in contact cannot understand why people do not respond to their efforts to sustain effective organizations, why people seemingly do not want to work, and why people want to leave apparently good organizations. Executives faced with these problems are often confused, angry, and hostile to their own people. The terms of office of chief executives, particularly those in educational and governmental administration, become shorter as the managerial, frustrations increase.

The crisis in motivation has long been evident to students of organization, and they have offered problem-plagued executives a wide range of theories to cope with it. Suffice it to say that, by this time, thousands of executives are familiar with these theories. Many have taken part in managerial grid training, group dynamics laboratories, seminars on the psychology of management, and a wide range of other forms of training. Some have run the full gamut of training experiences; others have embraced a variety of panaceas offered by quacks.

DISAPPOINTING REMEDIES

The results of the aforementioned theories have not been impressive. While some companies have put them into practice with a degree of success, most have either given up their efforts as too simplistic for the complexity of organizational phenomena or have simply failed in their attempts.

There are, of course, many reasons why the remedies have failed. For one thing, executives often feel unqualified to apply the concepts. And in that feeling they are frequently right. Managers who have had little or no previous exposure to the behavioral sciences, let alone any formal training in this area, can get only the barest introductory knowledge in a brief training program. An executive would not expect a person to be able to design a complex building after a week-long training program in architecture; yet both the executive and the people who train him often expect that he will be a different person after he attends a one-week sensitivity-training laboratory.

Furthermore, it is one thing to learn to become more aware of one's own feelings; it is quite another to do something different about managing them, let alone about managing those forces that affect the feelings of other people. If everyone who had experienced psychotherapy were by that fact an expert therapist, there would be no shortage of such healers. Experience is not enough; training in a conceptual framework and supervised skill practice is also required. Many executives who have expected more of themselves and of such training have therefore been disillusioned, despite the benefits that have often resulted from even such brief experiences.

Would longer training help? Not much. Unlike marketing executives who implement marketing programs, and experts who install financial control systems, behavioral scientists (with the exception of certain kinds of psychotherapists) are not themselves expert in *doing*. While many know about the theories, and some of them practice what is called organizational development, they do not themselves change organizations. Instead they usually help people to think through alternative action possibilities and overcome communications blocks to working out their own solutions. Since most behavioral scientists are not skilled in changing organizations, then, they are not in a position to teach executives how to change them.

Power and fear: Another reason why solutions to motivation problems do not work is that many executives are fearful of losing control of their organizations. The new theories have confronted executives with the need to distribute power in their organizations, which in turn raises questions about their authority and right to manage.

A recent study of 400 top executives in Europe indicates that they feel menaced by these new theories.[1] Most see themselves in the middle of an unsettling transition in management styles. They report that they can no longer use the authority of position; instead, they must gain their position by competition with subordinates and defend that position each step of the way. Of those interviewed, 61% spontaneously indicated that their primary problem is personnel management. Almost all of these executives have leadership problems.

Many businessmen are threatened when they must stimulate people to participate in making organizational decisions and invite people to express themselves more freely. When an executive's whole life thrust has been to obtain a position of power and control, he finds it particularly threatening to witness his power eroding as older methods of control and motivation become less effective.

Coupled with the fear of losing control is the fact that a disproportionate number of executives are characteristically insensitive to feelings. Some people, for example, pursue executive careers to obtain power over others as a way of compensating for real or fancied personal inadequacies, or as a reaction to an unconscious sense of helplessness. They are neurotically driven, and their single-minded, perpetual pursuit of control blinds them to their own subtle feelings and those of others.

Furthermore, many executives have engineering, scientific, legal, or financial backgrounds. Each of these fields places a heavy emphasis on cognitive rationality and measurable or verifiable facts. People who enter them usually are trained from childhood to suppress their feelings, to maintain a competitive, aggressive, nonemotional front. They are taught to be highly logical, and they seek to impose that kind of rationality on organizations.

As a result, they simply do not understand the power of people's feelings, and all too often they are incapable of sensing such feelings in everyday practice without considerable help. They are like tone-deaf people who, attending an opera, can understand the lyrics but cannot hear the music. Such executives are typified by a company president who was a participant in a seminar on psychological aspects of management. Halfway through the first lecture, he broke in to say, "You have already told me more about this subject than I want to know." Although he stayed to the end of the program, he simply could not grasp what was being taught.

All of these reasons, coupled with the inadequacies of contemporary motivational theory itself, explain much of the gap between theory and practice. In time, with new knowledge and better training experiences, most of the gap may be overcome. But the fact remains that much more effort could be applied now. This brings us to that unconscious assumption about motivation to which I referred earlier, one held particularly by executives in all types of organizations and reinforced by organizational theories and structures.

Fact and Fallacy

Frequently, I have asked executives this question: What is the dominant philosophy of motivation in American management? Almost invariably, they quickly agree that it is the carrot-and-stick philosophy, reward and punishment. Then I ask them to close their eyes for a moment, and to form a picture in their mind's eye with a carrot at one end and a stick at the other. When they have done so, I then ask them to describe the central image in that picture. Most frequently they respond that the central figure is a jackass.

If the first image that comes to mind when one thinks "carrot-and-stick" is a jackass, then obviously the unconscious assumption behind the reward-punishment model is that one is dealing with jackasses who must be manipulated and controlled. Thus, unconsciously, the boss is the manipulator and controller, and the subordinate is the jackass.

The characteristics of a jackass are stubbornness, stupidity, willfulness, and unwillingness to go where someone is driving him. These, by interesting coincidence, are also the characteristics of the unmotivated employee. Thus it becomes vividly clear that the underlying assumption which managers make about motivation leads to a self-fulfilling prophecy. People inevitably respond to the carrot-and-stick by trying to get more of the carrot while protecting themselves against the stick. This predictable phenomenon has led to the formation of unions, the frequent sabotage of management's motivation efforts, and the characteristic employee suspicion of management's motivational (manipulative) techniques.

Employees obviously sense the carrot-and-stick conception behind management's attitudes and just as obviously respond with appropriate self-defending measures to the communications built around those attitudes. Of course, there is much talk about the need to improve communication in organizations. All too often, however, the problem is not that communication is inadequate but, rather, that it is already too explicit in the wrong way. When employees sense that they are being viewed as jackasses, they will automatically see management's messages as manipulative, and they will resist them, no matter how clear the type or how pretty the pictures.

PERPETUAL POWER GAP

Since the turn of the century, numerous different philosophies of management have appeared, each emphasizing a different dimension of the management task and each advocating a new set of techniques. Although these philosophies differ from each other in many respects, all are based on reward-punishment psychology. For example, most of the contemporary psychological conceptions of motivation take a reward-punishment psychology for granted; they advocate trust and openness among employees and managers, but at the same time they acknowledge that the more powerful have a natural right to manipulate the less powerful.

As long as anyone in a leadership role operates with such a reward-punishment attitude toward motivation, he is implicitly assuming that he has (or should have) control over others and that they are in a jackass position with respect to him. This attitude is inevitably one of condescending contempt whose most blatant mask is paternalism. The result is a continuing battle between those who seek to wield power and those who are subject to it. The consequences of this battle are increased inefficiency, lowered productivity, heightened absenteeism, theft, and sometimes outright sabotage.

BUREAUCRATIC BADLANDS

The problems resulting from the jackass fallacy are compounded further by bureaucratic organizational structures. Such structures are based on a military model that assumes complete control of the organization by those at the top. In pure form, it is a rigid hierarchy, complete with detailed job descriptions and fixed, measurable objectives.

The bureaucratic structure requires everyone at every level to be dependent on those at higher levels. Hiring, firing, promotion, demotion, reassignment, and similar actions are the prerogatives of superiors who can make decisions unilaterally. In short, one's fate is decided by a distant "they" who are beyond his influence and control.

Under such circumstances, the subordinate person becomes increasingly defensive. He must protect himself against being manipulated and against the feeling of helplessness that inevitably accompanies dependency. Rank-and-file employees have long done so by unionization; managerial and professional employees are beginning to follow suit, and this trend will continue to grow.

While the bureaucratic structure, with its heavy emphasis on internal competition for power and position, is often touted as a device for achievement, it is actually a system for defeat. Fewer people move up the pyramidal hierarchy at each step. This leaves a residual group of failures, often euphemistically called "career people," who thereafter are passed over for future promotions because they have not succeeded in the competition for managerial positions.

Most of these people feel resentful and defeated. Often they have been manipulated or judged arbitrarily. They are no longer motivated by competitive spirit, because the carrots and the sticks mean less. There is little need, in their eyes, to learn more; they simply do as they are told. They usually stay until retirement unless they are among the "deadwood" that is cleaned out when a new management takes over.

Executives new to a company or a higher-level job like to think of themselves as being effective in cleaning out such deadwood or trimming the excess managerial fat. Some take to that task with great vigor. Unfortunately, the consequences are more negative than enthusiastic executives like to recognize. In one large company, for example, management hoped that the 40-year-olds would respond with unbridled enthusiasm when the 50-year-olds were cleaned out. But the younger men failed to respond, because they saw that what was happening to the older men would be their likely fate ten years hence.

Bureaucratic structure, with its implicit power-struggle orientation, increases infighting, empire building, rivalry, and a sense of futility. It tends to magnify latent feelings that the organization is a hostile environment which people can do little to change, and it bolsters the jackass fallacy. Little wonder that many young people do not want to get caught up in such situations! Since 90% of those who work do so in organizations, most young people, too, must do so. But they would rather be in organizations that provide them an opportunity to demonstrate their competence and proficiency than in organizations that test their ability to run a managerial maze successfully.

A FORMIDABLE CHALLENGE

The great jackass fallacy and the bureaucratic organization structure present major obstacles to organizational survival. They are essentially self-defeating if what an executive wants from employees is spontaneity, dedication, commitment, affiliation, and adaptive innovation.

As I have already indicated, many executives try to cope with the pathology of the system by introducing such new techniques as group dynamics and job enrichment. These are simply patches on the body politic of an organization. There is no way to integrate them effectively. When people are asked to express their feelings more freely and to take on greater responsibility, they soon come into conflict with power centers and power figures in a system geared to the acquisition of power. The latter soon cry, "Business is not a democracy," and disillusionment sets in once again, both on the part of managers who tried the new techniques and on the part of subordinates who were subjected to them.

Unless the fundamental assumptions of management (and behavioral scientists) about motivation are changed, and unless the organizational structure is altered to match these changed assumptions, the underlying jackass fallacy will remain visible to those who are subjected to it. Despite whatever practices the organization implements, people will avoid, evade, escape, deny, and reject both the jackass fallacy and the military-style hierarchy.

If the executive grasps the import of what I am saying, shudders uncomfortably, and wants to do something about the problem, what are his alternatives? Is he forever doomed to play with psychological gimmicks? Is he himself so much a victim of his assumptions that he cannot change them? I do not think that he necessarily is. There are constructive actions that he can take.

The First Steps

Anyone who supervises someone else should look carefully at the assumptions he is making about motivation. He must assess the degree to which carrot-and-stick assumptions influence his own attitudes. For example, an executive might argue that if he tried to be nice to people, the stick would be softened. But even then he would merely be exhibiting paternalistic kindness. As long as his assumptions about people remain unchanged, his "being nice" is only a disguised form of carrot-and-stick which seeks to increase loyalty by creating guilt in those who are the recipients of his managerial largesse. His first priority should be to change his way of thinking about people.

After honestly and frankly facing up to one's own assumptions about what makes people tick, the next step is to look at one's organizational structure. Most organizations are constructed to fit a hierarchical model. People assume that the hierarchical organizational structure is to organizations as the spine is to human beings, that it is both a necessity and a given. As a matter of fact, it is neither a necessity nor a given.

I am arguing not against the distribution of power and control, but, rather, that this distribution need not take one particular form. Every executive should ask himself: "Is my operation organized to achieve a hierarchical structure or is it structured to accomplish the task it must do?" If it is organized more to fit the model than to fit the task, he should begin exploring more appropriate organization models.[2] To do otherwise is to invite trouble—if it has not already started.

Conclusion

It is time for business leaders to enter a phase of more serious thinking about leadership and organizational concepts. They must do so on behalf of their own organizations as well as on behalf of society. The issue I have been discussing is critically important for society as a whole, because society increasingly is made up of organizations. The less effectively organizations carry out the work of society, the greater the cost in money and in social paralysis. The latter leads to the kind of demoralization already evident in organizations as well as in problems of transportation, health care delivery, education, and welfare.

Furthermore, we are in the midst of a worldwide social revolution, the central thrust of which is the demand of all people to have a voice in their own fate. Business leaders, many of whom have international interests and see the multiple facets of this thrust in a wide range of countries, should be in the forefront of understanding and guiding these social changes into productive channels. By applying new principles of motivation to their own organizations, they are in a position not only to sustain the vitality of those organizations but, more important, to keep them adaptive to changing circumstances.

In addition, the progressive changes that executives institute in their own organizations can then become the models for other institutional forms in a given culture. Not the least of the advantages of being on the frontier is that executives and corporations avoid the onus of being continuously compelled by angry or apathetic employees to change in ways which may be destructive to both the business and the people involved.

But leading is more than a matter of pronouncing clichés. Leading involves an understanding of motivation. It is to this understanding that business leaders must now dedicate themselves. And the way to start is by countering the great jackass fallacy in their own organizations.

Notes

1. Frederick Harmon, "European Top Managers Struggle for Survival," *European Business,* Winter 1971, p. 14.

2. Paul R. Lawrence and Jay W. Lorsch, *Organization and Environment: Managing Differentiation and Integration* (Boston, Division of Research, Harvard Business School, 1967).

Reprint 73106

Originally published in January–February 1973

9

Conflicts That Plague Family Businesses

The job of operating a family-owned company is often grievously complicated by friction arising from rivalries involving a father and his son, brothers, or other family members who hold positions in the business, or at least derive income from it. Unless the principals face up to their feelings of hostility, the author says, the business will suffer and may even die. He offers some advice on how relatives can learn to live with their peculiar situation. But he concludes that the only real solution is to move toward professional management.

In U.S. business, the most successful executives are often men who have built their own companies. Ironically, their very success frequently brings to them and members of their families personal problems of an intensity rarely encountered by professional managers. And these problems make family businesses possibly the most difficult to operate.[1]

It is obvious common sense that when managerial decisions are influenced by feelings about and responsibilities toward relatives in the business, when nepotism exerts a negative influence, and when a company is run more to honor a family tradition than for its own needs and purposes, there is likely to be trouble.

However, the problems of family businesses go considerably deeper than these issues. In this article I shall examine some of the more difficult underlying psychological elements in operating these businesses and suggest some ways of coping with them.

They Start with the Founder

The difficulties of the family business begin with the founder. Usually he is an entrepreneur for whom the business has at least three important meanings:

1. The entrepreneur characteristically has unresolved conflicts with his father, research evidence indicates. He is therefore uncomfortable when being supervised, and starts his own business both to outdo his father and to escape the authority and rivalry of more powerful figures.[2]

2. An entrepreneur's business is simultaneously his "baby" and his "mistress." Those who work with him and for him are characteristically his instruments in the process of shaping the organization.

   If any among them aspires to be other than a device for the founder—that is, if he wants to acquire power himself—he is soon likely to find himself on the outside looking in. This is the reason why so many organizations decline when their founders age or die.

3. For the entrepreneur, the business is essentially an extension of himself, a medium for his personal gratification and achievement above all. And if he is concerned about what happens to his business after he passes on, that concern usually takes the form of thinking of the kind of monument he will leave behind.

The fundamental psychological conflict in family businesses is rivalry, compounded by feelings of guilt, when more than one family member is involved. The rivalry may be felt by the founder—even though no relatives are in the business—when he unconsciously senses (justifiably or not) that subordinates are threatening to remove him from his center of power. Consider this actual case.

> An entrepreneur, whose organization makes scientific equipment and bears his name, has built a sizable enterprise in international markets. He has said that he wants his company to be noted all over the world for contributing to society.
>
> He has attracted many young men with the promise of rapid promotions, but he guarantees their failure by giving them assignments and then turning them loose without adequate organizational support. He intrudes into the young men's decision making, but he counterbalances this behavior with paternalistic devices. (His company has more benefits than any other I have known.)
>
> This technique makes his subordinates angry at him for what he

has done, then angry at themselves for being hostile to such a kind man. Ultimately, it makes them feel utterly inadequate. He can get people to take responsibility and move up into executive positions, but his behavior has made certain that he will never have a rival.

The conflicts created by rivalries among family members—between fathers and sons, among brothers, and between executives and other relatives—have a chronically abrasive effect on the principals. Those family members in the business must face to the impact that these relationships exert must learn to deal with them, not only for their emotional health but for the welfare of the business.

I shall consider in turn the father-son rivalry, the brother-brother rivalry, and other family relationships.

Father-Son Rivalry

As I have indicated, for the founder the business is an instrument, an extension of himself. So he has great difficulty giving up his baby, his mistress, his instrument, his source of social power, or whatever else the business may mean to him. Characteristically, he has great difficulty delegating authority and he also refuses to retire despite repeated promises to do so.

This behavior has certain implications for father-son relationships. While he consciously wishes to pass his business on to his son and also wants him to attain his place in the sun, unconsciously the father feels that to yield the business would be to lose his masculinity.

At the same time, and also unconsciously, he needs to continue to demonstrate his own competence. That is, he must constantly reassure himself that he alone is competent to make "his" organization succeed. Unconsciously the father does not want his son to win, take away his combination baby and mistress, and displace him from his summit position.

These conflicting emotions cause the father to behave inexplicably in a contradictory manner, leading those close to him to think that while on the one hand he wants the business to succeed, on the other hand he is determined to make it fail.

The son's feelings of rivalry are a reflection of his father's. The son naturally seeks increasing responsibility commensurate with his growing maturity, and the freedom to act responsibly on his own. But he is frustrated by his father's intrusions, his broken promises of retirement, and his self-aggrandizement.

The son resents being kept in an infantile role—always the little boy in his father's eyes—with the accompanying contempt, condescension, and lack of confidence that in such a situation frequently characterize the father's attitude. He resents, too, remaining dependent on his father for his income level and, as often, for title, office, promotion, and the other usual perquisites of an executive. The father's erratic and unpredictable behavior in these matters makes this dependency more unpalatable.

I have observed a number of such men who, even as company presidents, are still being victimized by their fathers who remain chairmen of the board and chief executive officers.

'WHY DON'T YOU LET ME GROW UP?'

Characteristically, fathers and sons, particularly the latter, are terribly torn by these conflicts; the father looks on the son as ungrateful and unappreciative, and the son feels both hostile to his father and guilty for his hostility.

The father bears the feeling that the son never will be man enough to run the business, but he tries to hide that feeling from his son. The son yearns for his chance to run it and waits impatiently but still loyally in the wings—often for years beyond the age when others in nonfamily organizations normally take executive responsibility—for his place on the stage.

If the pressures become so severe for him that he thinks of leaving, he feels disloyal but at the same time fears losing the opportunity that would be his if he could only wait a little longer. He defers his anticipated gratification and pleasure, but, with each postponement, his anger, disappointment, frustration, and tension mount. Here is a typical situation I know of.

> Matthew Anderson, a man who founded a reclaimed-metals business, has two sons. John, the elder, is his logical successor, but Anderson has given him little freedom to act independently, pointing out that, despite limited education, he (the father) has built the business and intuitively knows more about how to make it successful.
>
> Though he has told John that he wants him to be a partner, he treats John more like a flunky than an executive, let alone a succes-

sor. He pays the elder son a small salary, always with the excuse that he should not expect more because someday he will inherit the business. He grants minimal raises sporadically, never recognizing John's need to support his family in a style fitting his position in the company.

When John once protested and demanded both more responsibility and more income, his father gave Henry, the second son, a vice presidential title and a higher income. When Henry asked for greater freedom and responsibility, Anderson turned back to John and made him president (in name only). The father, as chairman of the board and chief executive officer, continued to second-guess John, excluded Henry from conferences (which of course increased John's feelings of guilt), and told John that Henry was "no good" and could not run the business.

Later, when John sought to develop new aspects of the business to avoid the fluctuations of the metals market, his father vetoed these ideas, saying, "This is what we know, and this is what we are going to do." He failed to see the possible destructive effects of market cycles on fixed overhead costs and the potential inroads of plastics and other cheaper materials on the reclaimed-metals business.

The upshot was that profits declined and the business became more vulnerable to both domestic and foreign (particularly Japanese) competition. When John argued with his father about this, he got the response: "What do you know? You're still green. I went through the Depression." Once again Anderson turned to Henry—making the black sheep white, and vice versa.

Angered, John decided to quit the business, but his mother said, "You can't leave your father; he needs you." Anderson accused him of being ungrateful, but he also offered to retire, as he had promised to do several times before.

Despite his pain, John could not free himself from his father. (Only an ingrate would desert his father, he told himself.) Also John knew that if he departed, he could not go into competition with his father, because that would destroy him. But John shrank from entering an unfamiliar business.

Nevertheless, from time to time John has explored other opportunities while remaining in the business. But each time his father has undercut him. For instance, John once wanted to borrow money for a venture, but Anderson told the bankers that his son was not responsible.

Now, when John is middle-aged, he and his father are still battling. In effect John is asking, "Why don't you let me grow up?" and his father is answering, "I'm the only man around here. You must stay here and be my boy."

'HE'S DESTROYING THE BUSINESS'

The son also has intense rivalry feelings, of course. These, too, can result in fierce competition with his father and hostile rejection of him, or abject dependence on him. Sometimes the competition can lead to a manipulative alignment with the mother against him. Consider this actual case.

Bill Margate, a recent business school graduate, knew that he would go into his father's electronic components business. But he decided that first he should get experience elsewhere, so he spent four years with a large manufacturing company. From his education and experience, he became aware of how unsophisticated his father was about running the business and set about showing the senior Margate how a business should be professionally managed.

Margate can do no right in Bill's eyes, at least not according to the books which he has read but which his father has never heard of. Bill frequently criticizes his father, showing him how ignorant he is. When Margate calls his son "green," Bill retorts, "I've forgotten more about managing a business than you'll ever know."

Bill's mother is also involved in the business; she has been at her husband's side for many years, though their relationship is less than the best. Mrs. Margate dotes on her son and complains to him about her husband, and she encourages Bill in his attacks on his father. When Bill undertook several ventures that floundered, she excused the failures as being caused by his father's interference.

But whenever the father-son battle reaches a peak, Mrs. Margate shifts allegiance and stands behind her husband. So the senior Margate has an ally when the chips are down, at the price of a constant beating until he gets to that point.

The struggle for the business has remained a stand-off. But as the elder Margate has grown older, his son's attacks have begun to tell on him. Bill has urged him to take long Florida vacations, but Margate refuses because he fears what would happen when his back is turned. For the same reason, he does not permit Bill to sign checks for the company.

Now Margate has become senile, and Bill's criticism of him continues, even in public. "He's destroying the business," Bill will say.

However, Bill cannot act appropriately to remove his father (even though he is now incompetent) because of his guilt feelings about his incessant attacks. That would destroy his father, literally, and he cannot bring himself to do it.

'THE OLD MAN REALLY BUILT IT'

The problem for the son becomes especially acute when and if he does take over. Often the father has become obsolete in his managerial conceptions. The organization may have grown beyond one man's capacity to control it effectively. That man may have been a star whose imagination, creativity, or drive are almost impossible to duplicate. He may also have been a charismatic figure with whom employees and even the public identified.

Whatever the combination of factors, the son is likely to have to take over an organization with many weaknesses hidden behind the powerful facade of the departed leader. For these reasons many businesses, at the end of their founders' tenure, fall apart, are pirated, or are merged into another organization.

The Ford Motor Company, at the demise of Henry Ford, was a case in point; a completely new management had to be brought in. Henry Ford II was faced with the uncomfortable task of having to regenerate a company that appeared to have the potential for continued success, but which, according to some, could easily have gone bankrupt.

While the son is acting to repair the organizational weaknesses left by his father, he is subject to the criticism of those persons who, envious of his position, are waiting for him to stumble. They "know" that he is not as good as his father. If he does less well than his father, regardless of whether there are unfavorable economic conditions or other causes, he is subject to the charge of having thrown away an opportunity that others could have capitalized on.

The scion cannot win. If he takes over a successful enterprise, and even if he makes it much more successful than anyone could have imagined, nevertheless the onlookers stimulate his feelings of inadequacy. They say, "What did you expect? After all, look what he started with." To illustrate.

Tom Schlesinger, the president of a restaurant chain, inherited the business after his father had built a profitable regional network of outlets with a widely known name—a model for the industry.

Tom has expanded it into nearly a national operation. He has done this with astute methods of finance that allow great flexibility, and with effective control methods that maintain meal quality and at the same time minimize waste. By any standards he has made an important contribution to the business.

But those who remember his father cannot see what Tom has done because the aura of his father still remains. They tend to minimize Tom's contribution with such observations as, "Well, you know, the old man really built that business."

Tom cannot change the attitude of those who knew his father, and he feels it is important to keep lauding his father's accomplishments in order to present a solid family image to employees, customers, and the community. But he is frustrated because he has no way of getting the world to see how well he has done.

Brother-Brother Rivalry

The father-son rivalry is matched in intensity by the brother-brother rivalry. Their competition may be exacerbated by the father if he tries to play the sons off against each other or has decided that one should wear his mantle, as I showed previously. (In my experience, the greatest difficulties of this kind occur when there are only two brothers in the organization.)

The problem is further complicated if their mother and their wives are also directly or indirectly involved in the business. Mothers have their favorites—regardless of what they say—and each wife, of course, has a stake in her husband's position. He can become a foil for his wife's fantasies and ambition.

The rivalry between brothers for their father's approval, which began in childhood, continues into adult life. It can reach such an intensity that it colors every management decision and magnifies the jockeying for power that goes on in all organizations. Consider this situation:

Arthur, five years older than his sibling, is president, and Warren is an operating vice president, of the medium-sized retailing organization which they inherited. To anyone who cares to listen, each maintains that he can get along very well without the other.

Arthur insists that Warren is not smart, not as good a businessman as he; that his judgment is bad; and that even if given the chance, he would be unable to manage the business.

Warren asserts that when the two were growing up, Arthur considered him to be a competitor, but for his part, he (Warren) did not care to compete because he was younger and smaller. Warren says that he cannot understand why his older brother has always acted as if they were rivals, and adds, "I just want a chance to do my thing. If he'd only let me alone with responsibility! But he acts as if the world would fall apart if I had that chance."

Every staff meeting and meeting of the board (which includes non-family members) becomes a battle between the brothers. Associates, employees, and friends back off because they decline to take sides. The operation of the organization has been turned into a continuous family conflict.

THE ELDER . . .

Ordinarily, the elder brother succeeds his father. But this custom reaffirms the belief of the younger brother (or brothers) that the oldest is indeed the favorite. In any event, the older brother often has a condescending attitude toward the younger. In their earliest years the older is larger, physically stronger, more competent, and more knowledgeable than the younger merely because of the difference in age, as in the case I just cited.

Only in rare instances does the younger brother have the opportunity to match the skills, competence, and experience of the elder until they reach adulthood. By that time the nature of this relationship is so well established that the older brother has difficulty regarding the younger one as adequate and competent.

Moreover, the eldest child is earlier and longer in contact with the parents, and their control efforts fall more heavily on him. Consequently, older children tend to develop stronger consciences, drive themselves harder, expect more of themselves, and control themselves more rigidly than younger ones. Being already, therefore, a harsh judge of himself, the eldest is likely to be an even harsher judge of his younger siblings.

. . . AND THE YOUNGER

The younger brother attempts to compensate for the effects of this childhood relationship and his older brother's efforts to control him by trying to carve out a place in the business that is his own. This he guards with great zeal, keeping the older brother out so he can demonstrate to himself, his brother, and others that he is indeed competent and has his own piece of the action for which he is independently responsible.

If the brothers own equal shares in the organization and both are members of the board, as is frequently the case, the problems are compounded. On the board they can argue policy from equally strong positions. However, when they return to operations in which one is subordinate to the other, the subordinate one, usually the junior brother, finds it extremely difficult to think of himself in a subservient role.

The younger one usually is unable to surmount this problem in their mutual relationship. He tends to be less confident than his brother and considers himself to be at a permanent disadvantage, always overcontrolled, always unheeded. Since the older brother views the younger one as being less able, he becomes involved in self-fulfilling prophecies. Distrusting his younger brother, he is likely to over-control him, give him less opportunity for freedom and responsibility—which in turn make for maturity and growth—and likely to reject all signs of the younger brother's increasing competence.

If for some reason the younger brother displaces the older one, and particularly if the latter becomes subordinate to him, the younger brother is faced with feelings of guilt for having attacked the elder and usurped what so often is accepted as the senior brother's rightful role.

Intrafamily Friction

The problems of the father and brothers extend to other relatives when they, too, become involved in the business. In some families it is expected that all who wish to join the company will have places there. This can have devastating effects, particularly if the jobs are sinecures.

The chief executive of a family business naturally feels a heavy responsibility for the family fortunes. If he does not produce a profit, the effect on what he considers to be his image in the financial markets may mean less to him than the income reduction which members of his family will suffer. So he is vulnerable to backbiting from persons whom he knows only too well and whom he cannot dismiss as faceless. Consider this case.

Three brothers started a knitting business. Only one of the brothers had sons, and only one of the those sons stayed in the business; he eventually became president. The stock is held by the family. Two widowed aunts, his mother, his female cousins (one of whom was already widowed), and his brother, a practicing architect, depend on the business for significant income.

When business is off, the women complain. If the president wants to buy more equipment, they resist. If they hear complaints from employees or merchant friends, they make these complaints known at family gatherings. The president is never free from the vixens who are constantly criticizing and second-guessing him.

Perhaps more critical for the health of the business are the factional divisions that spring up in the organization as associates and subordinates choose the family members with whom they want to be identified. (Often, however, those who take sides discover that in a crisis the family unites against "outsiders," including their partisans, who are then viewed as trying to divide the family.)

If the nonfamily employees or board members decide not to become involved in a family fight and withdraw from relations with its members until the conflict is resolved, the work of the organization may be paralyzed. Worse yet, the dispute may eventually embroil the entire organization, resulting in conflicts at the lowest levels, as employees try to cope with the quarrels thrust on them.

Now the business has become a battleground that produces casualties but no peace. Such internecine warfare constitutes a tremendous barrier to communication and frustrates adequate planning and rational decision making.

A business in which numerous members of the family of varying ages and relationships are involved often becomes painfully disrupted around issues of empires and succession. Its units tend to become family-member territories and therefore poorly integrated organizationally, if at all.

As for succession, the dominant or patriarchal leader may fully expect to pass on the mantle of leadership to other, elder relatives in their turn. He may even promise them leadership roles, particularly if he has had to develop a coalition to support his position.

But for both realistic and irrational reasons he may well come to feel that none of the family members is capable of filling the role. He cannot very well disclose his decision, however, without stirring conflict, and he cannot bring in outside managers without betraying his relatives or reneging on his promises. On the other hand, he fears what would happen if he died without having designated a successor.

He may decide that the only way out is to sell the business (at least each relative will then get his fair share). But that solution is costly—it signifies not only the loss of the business as a means of employment, but also the betrayal of a tradition and, inevitably, the dissolution of close family ties that have been maintained through the medium of the business.

Facing Up to It

What can be done about these problems?

Most entrepreneurial fathers seem unable to resolve their dilemma themselves. They tend to be rigid and righteous, finding it difficult to understand that there is another, equally valid point of view which they can accept without becoming weaklings. Well-meaning outsiders who try to help the father see the effects of his behavior and think seriously about succession usually find themselves rejected. Then they lose whatever beneficial influence they may have had on him.

Several approaches have worked well. In some instances, sons have told their fathers that they recognize how important it is to the father to run his own business, but it is just as important for them to have the opportunity to "do their own thing." They then establish small new ventures either under the corporate umbrella or outside it, without deserting their father.

In a variant of this approach, a father who heads a retail operation opened a store in a different community for each of his sons. They do their buying together, with appropriate variations for each community, and maintain a common name and format, but each son runs his own operation while the father continues to run his.

In still another situation, the father merged his company into a larger one. Each of his two sons then became president of a subsidiary, and the father started a new venture while serving as a policy guide to his sons.

THE SON'S ROLE

Whether such alternatives can work depends in part on how the son conducts himself. He must be honest with himself and consider his paternal relationship candidly. He must take steps like these:

- He must ask himself why he chose to go into the family business. Most sons will say it is because of the opportunity and the feelings of guilt if they had not done so. Often, however, the basic reason is that a powerful father has helped make his son dependent on him, and so his son is reluctant to strike out on his own.

   He rationalizes his reluctance on the basis of opportunity and guilt. Struggling with his own dependency, he is more likely to continue to fight his father in the business because he is still trying to escape his father's control.

- Having examined this issue, and recognizing whatever validity it may have for him, the son must realize how often his own feelings of rivalry and anger get in his way. The more intense the rivalry, the more determinedly he seeks to push his father from his throne and the more aggressively the latter must defend himself. The son must therefore refrain from attack.

- He must quietly and with dignity, as a mature man, apprise his father of the realities—that he needs an area of freedom and an independent medium to develop skills and responsibilities. He can do so within the company framework or, if that is not feasible, outside it. In his own self-interest, as well as the company's, he must be certain that he gets the opportunity.

- He must not allow himself to be played off against his brother, and he must not allow his guilt to be manipulated. By the same token, he himself must not become involved with others in manipulation.

- He must honestly recognize and respect his father's achievement and competence. To build a business is no mean task, and usually the father still has useful skills and knowledge. Furthermore, the son should recognize the powerful psychological meaning of the business to his father and not expect him to be rational about his relationship to it.

If the son is still unable to make choices about what he wants to do, then, despite his pain and his father's reluctance to seek help, he himself must do so. Only he can take the initiative to relieve his anguish. Here is an example of how a group of sons has taken the initiative:

In Boston, a group calling itself SOB's (Sons of the Boss) has been formed to encourage men in that position to talk over common problems and share solutions. After educating themselves about the psychological dimensions of their situation, the group will make it a practice from time to time to invite their fathers as a group to discuss their problems openly. Then fathers and sons will get together separately.

This procedure may enable fathers and sons to realize that their particular problems are not unique to themselves, and to obtain support from those in a similar predicament.

Another approach for a son would be to ask his father to read this article and then discuss it privately with a neutral third party of their choice, to develop a perspective on their feelings and behavior. Having done so, a father is then in a better position to talk with his son, in the presence of the third party.

The third person must use his good offices to subdue recrimination. At the same time he must foster the father's expression of his fears over losing control, being unneeded, and suffering rejection, as well as the son's concerns about being overcontrolled, infantilized, and exploited.

If meeting with the third party fails to help, the next step is consultation with a psychologist or psychiatrist. There are rare instances, usually when conflict becomes severe, in which father and son are willing to go to a professional together or separately. In such cases it is often possible for the father to begin to make compromises, learn to understand his and his son's motivations, and work out with him newly defined, more compatible roles. Usually, however, such an effort requires continued supportive work by the professional and strong desire on the part of both men to resolve their differences.

If all these measures fail, those who work with patriarchs must learn to tolerate their situation until the opportunity arises for a change.

FRATERNAL SPIRIT

With respect to the brother-brother conflict, it is important for brothers to see that in their relationship they recapitulate ancient rivalries, and to perceive clearly the psychological posture each assumes toward the other. Once they understand these two issues, they must talk together about them. They should try to discuss freely the fears, worries, anger, and disappointments caused by each other. They should also be able to talk about their affection for each other.

Since there is love and hate in all relationships, theirs cannot, by definition, be pure. They should not feel guilty about their anger with each other, but they do need to talk it out. Having done that, they then must consider how they can divide the tasks in the organization so that each will have a chance to acquire and demonstrate competence and work in a complementary relationship with the other.

A brother cannot easily be subordinate at one level and equal on another. If a brother is an operating executive subordinate to the other, he gets into difficulty when he tries to be an equal on the board of directors. If more than one brother is on the board, then only one, as a rule, should be an operating executive. Of course, such rules are unnecessary if the brothers work well together.

If the brothers still cannot resolve their conflicts, then it becomes necessary to seek professional aid. If that does not help, they should consider being in separate organizations. In such a case, the big problem is the guilt feelings which the departing brother is likely to have for deserting the other and the family business.

TOWARD PROFESSIONAL MANAGEMENT

Where there are multiple and complex family relationships and obligations in a company, and particularly problems about succession, the best solution is a transcendent one. The family members should form a trust, taking all the relatives out of business operations while enabling them to continue to act in concert as a family.

The trust could allot financial support to every member who desires it to develop new business ventures on behalf of the family, thus providing a business interest that replaces the previous operating activity. This also helps maintain family cohesion and preserve the family's leadership role in the community.

In general, the wisest course for any business, family or nonfamily, is to move to professional management as quickly as possible. Every business must define its overriding purpose for being, from which it derives its objectives. Within this planning framework, the business must have a system for appraising the degree to which it and its components are achieving the goals that have been set.

All organizations need to rear subordinates in a systematic manner, thus creating the basic condition for their own regeneration. I know of no family business capable of sustaining regeneration over the long term solely through the medium of its own family members.

Where there is conflict, or inadequately rationalized territories, members of the family should move up and out of operations as quickly as possible into policy positions. Such movement recognizes the reality of ownership but does not confuse ownership with management.

It also opens the opportunity for professionally trained managers to succeed to major operating roles, instead of having to go to other organizations as soon as they are ready for major responsibility. The more competitive the business situation, the more imperative such a succession pattern is.

More than others, the family members need to have their own outside activities from which they can derive gratification equal to what they can obtain in the company. Otherwise they will be unable to let go and will continue to be barriers to others. Moreover, they will make it difficult to recruit and develop young persons with leadership potential who, as they mature, will see the inevitable barriers.

A number of family businesses have handled these issues wisely and have become highly professional in their management. The Dayton-Hudson Corporation and E.I. du Pont de Nemours are examples. Family members in both organizations must compete for advancement on the same terms as nonfamily managers. This practice is reinforced, at least at Dayton-Hudson, by a thorough performance appraisal system which includes appraisal of the chairman and president by a committee of the board.

Concluding Note

It is very difficult to cope with the problems of the family business. That does not mean, however, that one should merely endure them. There is no point in stewing in anger and guilt, since chronic irritation is only self-flagellation. It solves no problems; it only increases anger and hostility and paves the way for explosion, recrimination, and impaired relations.

The family member can do something about such problems, as he can with any other. If reasonable steps to solve the problems do not work and he continues to feel bound to the organization, his problem is largely psychological. To free himself to make choices about what he wants to do, he must talk his feelings out with his rival in the organization, which is best done in the presence of a neutral third person. Sometimes professional help is necessary.

This will reduce sufficiently the intensity of the emotions generated by the problem, so that he can see possible alternatives more clearly and make choices more freely. That is better than the years of agitation that usually accompany such problems, unless of course the rival needs to expiate his guilt by continuing to punish himself. In that case, it is his problem and not necessarily that of the family business.

Notes

1. For two thoughtful views of the subject, see Robert G. Donnelley, "The Family Business," HBR July–August 1964, p. 93; and Seymour Tilles, "Survival Strategies for Family Firms," *European Business*, April 1970, p. 9.

2. See Orvis F. Collins, David G. Moore, and Darab B. Unwalla, *The Enterprising Man* (East Lansing, Michigan State University Bureau of Business Research, 1964).

Reprint 71206

Originally published March–April 1971

10
On Being a Middle-Aged Manager

Becoming middle aged is the commonplace but crisis event that all executives must face sooner or later. The key to the conflict is the word "middle." Once a man reaches the middle, he is inevitably on a descending path. The crisis which follows this seemingly sudden realization is a period of adaptation to shock. The man who fails to mature in this sense becomes a disease that afflicts his organization; the one who opts for wisdom becomes an organizational resource. Here the author examines both the personal and organizational implications of being a middle-aged manager, about which little has appeared in print.

For most men, attainment of executive rank coincides with the onset of middle age, that vast gulf which begins about 35 and endures until a man has come to terms with himself and his human fate (for no man matures until he has done so). It is the peak time of personal expansion, when a man lives most fully the combined multiple dimensions of his life. He has acquired the wisdom of experience and the perspective of maturity. His activity and productivity are in full flower; his career is well along toward its zenith. He is at the widest range of his travels and his contacts with others. He is firmly embedded in a context of family, society, career, and his own physical performance. His successes are models for emulation; his failures, the object lessons for others. He has become a link from the past to the future, from his family to the outside world, from those for whom he is organizationally responsible to those to whom he owes responsibility. In a word, he has it made.

And need it all come to a harsh and bitter end? *No.*

A man cannot alter his inevitable fate. But he can manage the way he comes to terms with it. If he does so, rather than simply letting events take their course, he can do much to prolong the richness of his life as well as his years.

Sophocles, who lived to be more than 90, wrote *Oedipus Rex* at 75 and *Oedipus et Colonus* at 89. Titian completed his masterpiece, "The Battle of Lepanto," at 95; he began work on one of the most famous paintings in the world, "The Descent from the Cross," when he was 97. Benjamin Franklin invented bifocals at 78. Benjamin Duggar, Professor of Plant Physiology and Botanical Economics at the University of Wisconsin, was removed at age 70 by compulsory retirement; he then joined the research staff of Lederle Laboratories and several years later gave mankind Aureomycin. At 90, Pablo Casals still played the cello as no other man ever had. Santayana, the philosopher, wrote his first novel, *The Last Puritan,* at 72. Carl Sandburg wrote *Remembrance Rock* at 70. Freud's activities continued into his 80's.

These men are the exceptions, of course. But the fact that many people can mature creatively indicates that there is indeed hope for all of us who are closer to 35. In this article I propose to examine some of the experiences of middle age and suggest ways of maintaining creative potential.

First, however, permit me a brief qualification. I am not arbitrarily splitting businessmen into under 35 and over 35. That would be unrealistic. The figure 35 is not fixed. It will waver, because I am using it here in the sense of a stage of life, not a birthday.

Indexes of Health

Behind the flowering of middle age, a critical physical and psychological turnaround process is occurring. This is reflected in indexes of health. Statistics from Life Extension Examiners indicate that specific symptoms—such as extreme fatigue, indigestion, and chest pains—rise sharply among young executives just moving into top management. Only one third of the symptoms found in the 31-to 40-year-old management group can be traced to an organic cause, the examiners report.[1] They suggest that these problems come about because of both the manner in which the men live and the state of mind in which they work.

PSYCHOLOGICAL FACTORS

While some explanations for this increase in symptoms are no doubt a product of the aging process itself, there are more pressing psychological forces. The British psychoanalyst, Elliott Jaques, contends that a peak in the death rate between 35 and 40 is attributable to the shock which follows the realization that one is inevitably on a descending path.[2] This produces what for most men is a transitory period of depression. Depression increases a person's vulnerability to illness. There is much medical evidence to indicate that physical illness is likely to occur more frequently and more severely in people who feel depressed.

Lee Stockford of the California Institute of Technology reports from a survey of 1,100 men that about 5 out of 6 men in professional and managerial positions undergo a period of frustration in their middle 30's, and that 1 in 6 never fully recovers from it. Stockford attributes the crisis to a different kind of frustration: "This is the critical age—the mid-30's—when a man comes face to face with reality and finds that reality doesn't measure up to his dreams."[3]

A number of factors in executive work life contribute to the intensification of these feelings and the symptoms which result:

Increasing contraction of the hard work period—The average age at which men become company presidents is decreasing. As it does, the age span during which success can be achieved becomes narrower. The competitive pace therefore becomes more intense. It is further intensified by devices such as management by objectives and performance appraisals which give added impetus to the pressures for profit objectives.

Inseparability of life and career patterns—For managerial men in an intensely competitive career pattern, each year is a milepost. Time in job or level is a critical variable. If one does not move on time, he loses out on experience, position, and above all, the reputation for being a star. This means there necessarily must be repetitive subpeaks of anxiety around time dimensions.

Continuous threat of defeat—When both internal and external pressures for achievement are so high, the pain of defeat—always harsh—can be devastating, no matter how well a man seems to take it. Animal research indicates that when males are paired in combat, up to

80% of the defeated ones subsequently die although their physical wounds are rarely severe enough to cause death. We cannot generalize from animals to humans, but we can get some suggestion of the physical cost of the experience of personal defeat. When we turn back to the management pyramid and the choices which have to be made, obviously many men experience defeat, and all must live with the threat.

Increase in dependency—To cope with competition, the executive, despite his misgivings, must depend on specialists whose word he has to accept because of his lack of specialized knowledge. In fact, John Kenneth Galbraith advanced the thesis in *The New Industrial State* that the technical infrastructure of an organization really makes the decisions, leaving only pro forma approval for the executive.[4] The specialists have their own concepts, jargon, and motivation which often differ from those of the executive. Every executive wants to make good decisions. He is uneasy about decisions based on data he does not fully understand, gathered by people he does not fully understand, and presented in terms he does not fully understand. He is therefore often left to shudder at the specter of catastrophe beyond his control.

Denial of feelings—Commitment to executive career goals requires self-demand and self-sacrifice, and simultaneously inhibits close, affectionate relationships. One cannot allow himself to get close to those with whom he competes or about whom he must make decisions, or who are likely to make decisions about him. Often he bears a burden of guilt for the decisions he must make about others' careers.[5] No matter how strongly a man wants the achievement goals, he still has some feelings of anger, toward both himself and the organization which demands that sacrifice, for having to give up other desirable life goals. He must hold in tightly these feelings of anger, together with the feelings of affection and guilt, if they are unacceptable to him or in his business culture. Repressed feelings must continuously be controlled, a process which requires hyper-alertness and therefore energy.

Constant state of defensiveness—The pursuit of executive success is like playing the children's game, "King of the Hill." In that game, each boy is vying for the place at the top of the stump, fence, barrel, or even literally, the hill. All the others try to push the incumbent from his summit perch. Unlike the game, in executive life there is no respite.

Given this state of affairs, together with the other conditions to which I have just referred, one must be always "at the ready," as the military put it. To be at the ready psychologically means that one's whole body is in a continuing emergency state, with resulting greater internal wear and tear.

Shift in the prime-of-life concept—Western societies value youth. It is painfully disappointing to have attained a peak life stage at a time in history when that achievement is partially vitiated by worship of youth, when there is no longer as much respect for age or seniority. This is compounded by one's awareness of the decline of his physical capacities. Thus, at the height of a manager's attainment, he is likely to feel also that he has only partly made it, that he has already lost part of what he sought to win. Since only rarely can one have youth and achievement at the same time, there is something anticlimactic about middle-age success.

Subtle Changes

The issues having to do with health are only one facet of the middle-aging process. There are also subtle, but highly significant, changes in (1) work style, (2) point of view, (3) family relationships, and (4) personal goals. Let us look at each of these in turn.

WORK STYLE

Both the mode and the content of the work of creative men differ in early adulthood, or the pre-35 stage, from that of mature adulthood, or the post-35 stage. Jaques pointed this out when he observed:

> "The creativity of the 20's and early 30's tends to be a hot-from-the-fire creativity. It is intense and spontaneous, and comes out ready-made. . . . Most of the work seems to go on unconsciously. The conscious production is rapid, the pace of creation often being dictated by the limits of the artist's capacity physically to record the words or music he is expressing. . . . By contrast, the creativity of the late 30's and after is sculptured creativity. The inspiration may be hot and intense. The unconscious work is no less than before. But there is a big step between the first effusion of inspiration and the finished creative product. The inspiration itself may come more slowly. Even if

there are sudden bursts of inspiration they are only the beginning of the work process."[6]

Jaques adds that the inspiration for the older man is followed by a period of forming and fashioning the product, working and reworking the material, and acting and reacting to what has been formed. This is an experience which may go on for a period of years. The content of work changes, too, from a lyrical or descriptive content to one that is tragic and philosophical, followed by one that is serene. Jaques recalls that Shakespeare wrote his early historical plays and comedies before he was 35, his tragedies afterward.

Contrary to popular misconception, creativity does not cease at an early age. It is true that creative men have made major contributions before 40, but it is equally true that those who demonstrated such creativity continued to produce for many years thereafter. In fact, both in the arts and in the sciences, the highest output is in the 40's.

Executives have many of the same kinds of experiences as artists and scientists. Executives report the greatest self-confidence at 40. Though their instrumentality is the organization, younger and older men do different creative work with organizations. The younger man is more impulsive, flashy, and star-like with ideas; the older man is more often concerned with building and forming an organization. A conspicuous example is the hard-hitting company founder who, to the surprise of his organization, becomes less concerned with making money and more preoccupied with leaving an enduring company. Suddenly, he is talking about management development.

POINT OF VIEW

Concurrent with the shift in work style or orientation is a shift in point of view. This occurs in political and social thinking as well as in business. It is a commonplace that most people become more conservative as they grow older. It is an unspoken commonplace that they are more bored.

True, many activities are intrinsically boring and become more so with repetition, but others no longer hold interest when one's point of view has changed.

DISILLUSIONMENT. Some of the boredom results from disillusionment. Early idealism, the tendency toward action, and the conviction of the innate goodness in people are in part a denial of the inevitable. Young people in effect say, "The world can be rosy. I'll help make it that way. People can be good to each other if only someone will show them how or remove the conditions which cause their frustration."

But in mid-life it becomes clear that people are not always good to each other; that removing the conditions of frustration does not always lead to good, friendly, loving behavior; and that people have a capacity for being ugly and self-destructive as well as good. One evidence for the denial of disillusionment is the effort in so many companies to keep things "nice and quiet." Such companies are characterized by the inability to accept conflict as given and conflict resolution as a major part of the executive's job.

OBSOLESCENCE. Another factor in change in point of view has to do with the feeling of becoming increasingly obsolescent. The middle-ager feels himself to be in a world apart from the young—emotionally, socially, and occupationally. This is covered today by the cliché "generation gap." But there is something real to the distance because there is a tendency to feel that one cannot keep up with the world no matter how fast he runs. Thus the sense of incompetence, even helplessness, is magnified. Some of this is reflected in an attitude that middle-aged executives often take.

For example, I once addressed the 125 members of the upper management group of a large company. When I finished, I asked them to consider three questions in the discussion groups into which they were going to divide themselves:

1. Of what I had said, what was most relevant to their business?
2. Of what was most relevant, what order of priority ought to be established?
3. Once priority was established, who was to do what about the issues?

They handled the first question well when they reported back; none had difficulty specifying the relevant. They had a little more difficulty with the second. None touched the third; it was as if they felt they were not capable of taking the action with which they had been charged.

VOCATIONAL CHOICE. This incident might be excused on a number of bases if it were not for other unrelated or corroborative evidence which reflects a third dimension in our consideration of change in point of view. Harvard psychologist Anne Roe did a series of studies on vocational choice in the adult years. In one study she was trying to find out how people make decisions about selecting jobs.

"The most impressive thing about these interviews," she reports, "was how few of our subjects thought of themselves as considering alternatives and making decisions based on thoughtful examination of the situation. . . . They seemed not to recognize their role as chooser or their responsibility for choices. It was, indeed, this last aspect we found most depressing. Even among the executives, we find stress on contingencies and external influences more often than not."[7]

PAIN OF RIVALRY. The sense of being more distant from the sources of change, from the more impulsive agents of change, and of not being a chooser of one's fate spawns feelings of helplessness and inadequacy. This sense of remoteness is further magnified, as I have already noted, by feelings of rivalry. For boys, playing "King of the Hill" may be fun. For men, the greater the stakes and the more intense the motivation to hold one's place, the more threatening the rivals become. Yet, in the midst of this competitive environment, one is required to prepare his rivals to succeed him and ultimately to give way. The very name of the game is "Prepare Your Successor."

I recall a particular corporate situation in which the president had to decide who was to be executive vice president. When he made his choice, some of his subordinates were surprised because, they said, the man he picked was the hottest competitor for the president's job and usually such men were sabotaged. The surprising part of the event, as far as I was concerned, was not the choice, but the fact that the subordinates themselves had so clearly seen what tends to happen to rivals for the executive suite. It is indeed difficult to tolerate a subordinate when the executive senses himself to be, in any respect, on a downward trail while the subordinate is obviously still on his way up and just as obviously is demanding his place in the corporate sun.

This phenomenon is one of the great undiscussed dilemmas of the managerial role. Repeatedly, in seminars on psychological aspects of management, cases refer to executives who cannot develop others, particularly men that have nothing to fear, in the sense that their future security is assured and they still have upward avenues open to them. What is not seen, let alone understood, in such cases is the terrible pain of rivalry in middle age in a competitive business context that places a premium on youth. This paragraph from Budd Schulberg's *Life* review of *Thalberg: Life and Legend* captures the rivalry issue in one pointed vignette:

"There was to be a dramatic coda to the Irving Thalberg Story: the inevitable power struggle between the benevolent but jealous L.B. Mayer and the protégé he 'loved like a son.' Bitter was the conflict between Father and Son fighting over the studio's Holy Ghost. They fought over artistic decisions. They fought over separation of authorities. They fought over their division of the spoils, merely a symbol of power, for by now both were multi-millionaires. It was as if the old, tough, crafty beachmaster L.B. was determined to drive off the young, frail but stubborn challenger who dared ask Mayer for an equal piece of the billion-dollar action."[8]

In this case, the rivalry was evident in open conflict. It could be with men at that level and in that culture. However, in most cases, if the rivalry does not go on unconsciously, it is carefully disguised and rationalized. Executives are reluctant to admit such feelings even to themselves. Therefore, much of the rivalry is unconscious. The parties are less aware of why they are quarreling, or perhaps they are more aware of the fact that they never seem to settle their quarrels. Every executive can test such feelings in his own experience by reviewing how he felt when a successor took his place, even though he himself moved up, particularly when that successor changed some of his cherished innovations.

Thus it is difficult for each of us to see the unconscious battle he wages with subordinates, now wanting them to succeed, now damned if they will. Subordinates, however unable they are to see this phenomenon in themselves, can usually see it quite clearly in the behavior of the boss. But then there are few upward performance appraisals to help make such behavior conscious, and the behavior itself indicates to the subordinate that the rival would do well to keep his mouth shut.

DOSE OF ANGER. The change in point of view which throws such problems into relief and intensifies fear (though rarely do executives speak of fear) is compounded further by a significant dose of anger. It is easy to observe the anger of the middle-aged executive toward today's youth—who have more money, more opportunity, and more sex than was available yesterday. There is anger, too, that the youngsters are free to "do their thing" while today's executives, pressed by the experiences of the depression and the constraints of their positions, sometimes find it hard to do what they really want to do.

The anger with youth is most often expressed as resentment because "they want to start at the top" or "they aren't willing to wait their turn or get experience" or "they only want young ones around here now."

It is further reflected in such simultaneously pejorative and admiring descriptive nouns as "whiz kids," "jets," and "stars." These mixed-feeling phrases bespeak self-criticism and betrayal.

Every time the middle-aged manager uses such a phrase, he seems also to be saying that he has not done as well or that he has been under-cut. He who had to learn how to size up the market from firsthand contact with customers finds that knowledge now useless, replaced by a computer model constructed by a man who never canvassed a customer. He who thought business to be "practical" and "hardheaded" now finds that he must go back to school, become more intellectual, think ahead conceptually, or he is lost. The kids have outflanked him. They have it so good, handed to them on a platter, at his expense.

Older generations have always complained that the youth not only are unappreciative of their efforts, but take for granted what they have I struggled so hard to achieve. Nevertheless, management has never taken seriously the impact of such feelings on executive behavior. The result is an expensive loss of talent as it becomes apparent to young people that managements promise them far more than companies deliver.

I am certain in my own mind that it is the combination of rivalry and anger which makes it so difficult to create challenging ways to use young people in management. (Certainly it is not the dearth of problems to be tackled.) That in turn accounts for much of the astronomical turnover of young college graduates in their first years in a company and also for much of their subsequent disillusionment with managerial careers.

FAMILY RELATIONSHIPS

The same narrowing which occurs in the cycle of achievement in business has also been taking place within the family. People are marrying at earlier ages, children are being born earlier in the marriage and therefore leaving their parents earlier. In turn, the parents live alone with each other longer (according to latest census figures, an average of 16 years). This poses several problems which come to a head in middle life. By this point in time one usually has lost both his parents. Though he may have been independent for many years, nevertheless for the first time he feels psychologically alone.

Because an executive can less readily establish close friendships at work, and his mobility makes it difficult for him to sustain them in his off-work relationships, he tends to have greater attachment to his children. He therefore suffers greater loss when they leave home, and he usually does not compensate for these losses any more than he actively compensates for the loss of old friendships through death and distance.

His heavy commitment to his career and his wife's to the children tend to separate them from each other—a problem which is obscured while their joint focus is on the children. When the children leave home, he is left with the same conscious reasons for which he married her as the basis for the marriage (attractiveness, charm, liveliness) and often the same unconscious ones (a substitute for mother, anything but like mother, a guaranteed nonequal, and other, similarly unflattering, reasons).

But she is no longer the young girl he married. She has aged, too, and may no longer be her ideal sylph-like self of twenty years before. If, in addition, his unconscious reasons for marrying her are now no longer as important as they were earlier, there is little left for the marriage unless the couple has worked out another basis for mutual usefulness.

Meanwhile, for most couples there has been a general decrease in satisfaction with each other, less intimacy, a decline in frequency of sexual intercourse, and fewer shared activities. Wives become more preoccupied with their husbands' health because age compels them to unconsciously rehearse for widowhood. Husbands sense this concern and the reasons (which sometimes include a wish for widowhood) for it, and withdraw even more. This is part of what increases the sense of loneliness mentioned earlier, in the context of the need for greater closeness. These factors contribute to the relatively new phenomenon of the "twenty-year" divorce peak.

PERSONAL GOALS

Up to approximately age 45, creative executive effort is largely self-centered. That is, one is concerned with his achievement and his personal needs. After age 45, he turns gradually to matters outside himself. As psychologist Else Frenkel-Brunswik has shown, he becomes more concerned with ideals and causes, derived from religious or parental values.[9] He also becomes more concerned with finding purpose in life.

For example, a young executive, a "jet" in his company, became a subsidiary president early. And while in that role he became involved in resolving racial problems in his community. Although still president, and likely to be promoted to head the whole corporation, his heart is now in the resolution of community problems. Similarly, another executive has retired early to become involved in conservation. Still others leave business for politics, and not a few have become Episcopal priests.

As part of this change (which goes on unconsciously), there are periods of restlessness and discomfort. There appears to be a peak in travel between the ages of 45 and 50, and also a transitory period of loneliness as one leaves old, long-standing moorings and seeks others.

The restlessness and discomfort have another source. When the middle-aged manager is shifting his direction, he must necessarily use psychological energy for that task. As a consequence, it is more difficult to keep ancient, repressed conflicts under control. This is particularly true when the manager has managed to keep certain conflicts in check by promising himself he would one day deal with them. As he begins to feel that time is running out and that he has not delivered on his promises to himself, he begins to experience intense internal frustration and pressure. Sometimes he will try to hide such conflicts under a contemporary slogan like "identity crisis."

Not long ago, a 42-year-old executive told me that despite his age, his professional engineering training, and his good position, he was still having an identity problem. He said he really did not know what he wanted to do or be. A few questions quickly revealed that he would prefer to be in his own business. However, the moment we touched that topic, he was full of excuses and wanted to turn away from it. He did indeed know what he wanted to do; he was simply afraid to face it. He wanted to be independent but he could not break away from the security of his company. He had maintained the fantasy that he might some day, but as the passing years made that less likely, his conflict increased in intensity.

Most men will come nowhere near doing all they want to do with their lives. All of us have some degree of difficulty and frustration as a result. We become even more angry with ourselves when the prospect arises that time will run out before we have sampled, let alone savored, much of what there is in the world. But most of us subtly turn our efforts to meeting those ideal requirements.

The important point in all this is that, as psychologist Charlotte Buhler points out, it relates directly to survival.[10] The evidence indicates that a person's assessment as to whether he did or did not reach fulfillment has more to do with his old-age adjustment than literal loss of physical capacities and insecurity. Put another way, if a man has met his own standards and expectations reasonably well, he adapts more successfully to the aging process. If not, the converse holds: while experiencing the debilitation of aging, he is also simultaneously angry with himself for not having done what he should have. Anger with self is the feeling of depression. We have already noted the implications of depression for physical illness.

Significant Implications

Up to this point, we have been looking at the critical physical and psychological symptoms of the aging process. Now let us turn to the personal and organizational implications in all this.

FACING THE CRISIS

First, all of us must face up to the fact that there is such an event in men's lives as middle-age crisis. It is commonplace; it need not be hidden or apologized for. It frequently takes the form of depressive feelings and psychosomatic symptoms as well as increased irritability and discontent, followed by declining interest in and efforts toward mastering the world.

There is a premature tendency to give in to fate, to feel that one can have no choice about what happens to him, and, in effect, to resign oneself to the vagaries of chance. This period is essentially a mourning experience: regret, sorrow, anger, disappointment for something which has been lost—one's precious youth—and with it the illusion of omnipotence and immortality. It is necessary to be free to talk about the loss, the pain, and the regret, and even to shed a tear, literally or figuratively. We do indeed die a bit each day; we have a right to be shaken by the realization when we can no longer deny it.

When a middle-aged manager begins to experience such feelings, and particularly if they begin to interfere with his work or his enjoyment of life, he should talk to someone else about them, preferably a good counselor. This kind of mourning is far better than increasing the intense pace of running in an effort to escape reality. In the process of talking, the wise man reworks his life experiences and his feelings until he is all mourned out and no longer afraid of being mortal.

When a manager can take his own life transitions and his feelings about them seriously, he has the makings of maturity. In the course of making wine, after the grapes are pressed, the resulting liquid is left to age. In a sense, it continues to work. In the process of aging, it acquires body, color, and bouquet—in short, its character.

Like wine, people who work over their feelings about the aging process acquire a certain character with age. They deepen their awareness of themselves and others. They see the world in sharper perspective and with greater tolerance. They acquire wisdom. They love more, exploit less. They accept their own imperfection and therefore their own contributions. As Jaques has put it, "The successful outcome of mature creative work lies thus in constructive resignation both to the imperfections of men and to shortcomings in one's work. It is this constructive resignation which then imparts serenity to life and work."[11]

The middle-aged manager who fails to take himself, his crises, and his feelings seriously keeps running, intensifies his exploitation of others, or gives up to exist on a plateau. Some managers bury themselves more deeply in their work, some run after their lost youth with vain cosmetic efforts, others by chasing women, and still others by pursuing more power. A man's failure to mature in this sense then becomes a disease that afflicts his organization. He loses his people, his grasp of the realities of his life, and can only look back on the way it used to be as the ideal.

The executive who denies his age in these ways also denies himself the opportunity to prepare for what is to come, following some of the suggestions I shall discuss in the next section. He who continues to deny and to run will ultimately have to face emptiness when he can no longer do either and must still live with himself. The wise man will come to terms with reality early: he will take seriously the fact that his time is limited.

TAKING CONSTRUCTIVE ACTION

Second, a man must act. Only he who acts on his own behalf is the master of himself and his environment. Too many people accept what is for what will be. They most often say, "I can't do anything about it." What they really mean is that they won't do anything. Check your own experience. How often do you mean "won't" when you say "can't"? Much of psychotherapeutic effort is directed to helping people see how they have trapped themselves this way. There are indeed alternatives in most situations. Our traps are largely self-made.

There are a number of fruitful avenues for action in both personal and business life. In personal terms, the most important efforts are the renegotiation of the marriage and the negotiation of new friendships. Husband and wife might wisely talk out their accumulated differences, their disappointments and mutual frustrations as well as their wishes and aspirations. As they redefine their marriage contract, they clarify for themselves their interdependence or lack of it. If they remain silent with each other or attack in their frustration, they run the danger of falling apart in their anger at the expense of their need for each other.

In social terms, the executive must make a formal effort to find and cultivate new friends with a particular emphasis on developing companionship. We know from studies of concentration camp survivors and of the process of aging that those who have companions cope most effectively with the traumas of life. Those who do not almost literally die of their loneliness. As a man becomes less self-centered, he can devote more energy to cultivating others. When he individualizes and cultivates the next person, he creates the conditions for others' recognition of him as a person.

In public terms, the executive must become future oriented, but this time in conceptions that go beyond himself and his job. He invests himself in the future when he becomes actively involved in some ongoing activity of social value which has enduring purpose. Hundreds of schools, colleges, hospitals, and community projects—most of them obscure—await the capable man who gives a damn and wants that damn to matter. Most executives need not look more than a few blocks beyond their offices for such opportunities.

In business terms, the executive should recognize that at this point in time he ideally should be exercising a different kind of leadership and dealing with different organization problems. In middle age, the stage Erik Erikson has called "the period of generativity,"[12] if he opts for wisdom, he becomes an organizational resource for the development of others. His wisdom and judgment give body to the creative efforts of younger men. They help turn impulse into reality, and then to shape and reshape it into a thousand useful products and services. They offer those characteristics in an executive to be admired and emulated. He shifts from quarterback to coach, from day-to-day operations to long-range planning. He becomes more consciously concerned with what he is going to leave behind.

ORGANIZING FOR RENAISSANCE

Third, organizations must take the middle-age period seriously in their thinking, planning, and programming. I know of no organization—business, university, church, or hospital—which does. No one knows how much effectiveness is lost.

If one of the needs for coping with middle-age stress is the opportunity to talk about it, then part of every supervisory and appraisal counseling should be devoted to some of the issues and concerns of this state. Company physicians or medical examining centers should provide time for the patient to talk with the doctor about the psychological aspects of his age and his life. Sessions devoted to examining how groups are working together should, if they are middle-aged groups, have this topic on the agenda. Company educational programs should inform both men and their wives about this period and its unique pressures. Personnel counselors should give explicit attention to this issue in their discussions.

Obviously, there should be a different slant to executive or managerial training programs for men over 35 than for those under 35. Pre-35 programs should be geared to keeping the younger men "loose." They should be encouraged to bubble, to tackle old problems afresh. This is not the time to indoctrinate men with rules and procedures, but rather to stimulate them toward their own horizons. Training challenges should be around tasks requiring sparkle, flashes of insight, and impulsive action.

Developmental programs for men over 35 should be concentrated largely on refreshment, keeping up, and conceptualization of problems and the organization. Tasks and problems requiring reorganization, reformulation, refining, and restructuring are tasks for men whose psychological time it is to rework. Brilliant innovative departures are unlikely to come from such men, except as they are the fruition of a lifetime of ferment, as was the *aggiornamento* of Pope John XXIII.

For them, instead, more attention should be given to frequent respites from daily organizational chores to get new views, to examine and digest them in work groups, and to think of their application to organizational problems and issues. When they move toward the future, they are likely to go in protected steps, like the man crawling on ice who pushes a plank before him. Pushing them hard to be free of the plank will tend to paralyze them into inaction. Rather, training programs should specifically include small experimental attempts to apply new skills and views with minimum risk.

Much of managerial training for these men should be focused on how to rear younger men. This means not only emphasis on coaching, counseling, teaching, and supporting, but also time and opportunity to talk about their feelings of rivalry and disappointment, to ventilate their anger at the young men who have it so good—the whole world at their feet and no place to go but up. Finally, it should include the opportunity for them to recognize, understand, and accept their uniquely human role. Instead of rejecting the younger men, they can then more comfortably place their bets and cheer their favorites on. In the youngsters' winning, they, too, can win.

For the executive, his subordinates, and the company, middle age can truly be a renaissance.

Notes

1. "Clinical Health Age: 30–40," *Business Week,* March 3, 1956. p. 56.
2. Elliott Jaques, "Death and the Mid-Life Crisis." *The International Journal of Psychoanalysis,* October 1965, p. 502
3. Unpublished.
4. Boston, Houghton Mifflin Company, 1967.
5. See "Management by Guilt" (Chapter 18) in my book *Emotional Health: in the World of Work* (New York, Harper & Row, 1964).
6. Jaques, op. cit., p. 503.
7. Anne Roe and Rhoda Baruch, "Occupational Changes in the Adult Years," *Personnel Administration,* July–August 1967, p. 32.
8. *Life,* February 28, 1969, p. 6.
9. "Adjustments and Reorientation in the Course of the Life Span," in *Middle Age and Aging,* edited by Bernice L. Neugarten (Chicago, the University of Chicago Press, 1968), p. 81.
10. Quoted in Raymond G. Kuhlen, "Developmental Changes in Motivation During the Adult Years," in Bernice L. Neugarten, op. cit., p. 134.
11. Jaques, op. cit., p. 505.
12. *Childhood and Society* (New York, W.W. Norton & Company, Inc., 1964), p.13.

Reprint 69406

Originally published July–August 1969

Index

About the Author

Harry Levinson, PhD, was the founder of The Levinson Institute. He is a clinical professor of psychology emeritus in the Department of Psychiatry, Harvard Medical School and a consultant to and lecturer for many business, academic, and government organizations. He received the Perry L. Rohrer Consulting Psychology Practice Award for outstanding achievement in psychological consultation in 1984; was recognized with the Massachusetts Psychological Association's Career Award and the first award of The Society of Psychologists in Management in 1985; received the Organization Development Professional Practice Award for Excellence from the American Society for Training and Development in 1988; was recognized with the I. Arthur Marshall Distinguished Alumnus Award of The Menninger Alumni Association in 1990; and was named corecipient of the American Psychological Association Award for Distinguished Professional Contributions to Knowledge in 1992. Dr. Levinson is past president of the American Board of Professional Psychology, past president of the Kansas Psychological Association, and former chairman of the Kansas Advisory Committee to the United States Civil Rights Commission.

Dr. Levinson is the author of many articles and books. He is the senior author of *Men, Management, and Mental Health* and author of *Emotional Health in the World of Work; Executive Stress; Executive* (a revision of *The Exceptional Executive*, which won the McKinsey Foundation, Academy of Management, and James A. Hamilton College of Hospital Administrators awards); *Organizational Diagnosis; The Great Jackass Fallacy;*

Psychological Man; *Casebook for Psychological Man*; and *Casebook for Psychological Man: Instructor's Guide*. With Dr. Stuart Rosenthal, he wrote *CEO: Corporate Leadership in Action* (which won The American College of Healthcare Executives–James A. Hamilton Book Award in 1986). He is also the author of *Ready, Fire, Aim: Avoiding Management by Impulse* and *Career Mastery* and the editor of *Designing and Managing Your Career*.

Dr. Levinson dedicates this volume to his wife Miriam, steadfast supporter and loving partner.